Shooting Blanks

Shooting Blanks

Facts Don't Matter to the Gun Ban Crowd

Alan Gottlieb
and
Dave Workman

Merril Press
Bellevue, Washington

Shooting Blanks is published by

Merril Press, P.O. Box 1682, Bellevue, WA 98009.

www.merrilpress.com

Phone: 425-454-7009

Distributed to the book trade by

Midpoint Trade Books, 27 W. 20th Street, New York, N.Y. 10011

www.midpointtradebooks.com

Phone: 212-727-0190

FIRST EDITION

LIBRARY OF CONGRESS CATALOGING-IN-PUBLICATION DATA

GOTTLIEB, ALAN M.
    SHOOTING BLANKS : FACTS DON'T MATTER TO THE GUN BAN CROWD / ALAN GOTTLIEB AND DAVE WORKMAN.
        P. CM.
    ISBN 978-0-936783-63-5
    1. GUN CONTROL--UNITED STATES. 2. FIREARMS--UNITED STATES. 3. FIREARMS--LAW AND LEGISLATION--UNITED STATES. I. WORKMAN, DAVE. II. TITLE.
    HV7436.G6759 2011
    363.330973--DC23
                                    2011033370

PRINTED IN THE UNITED STATES OF AMERICA

Dedicated to all those
anti-gun rights activists
and organizations that
consistently shoot off their mouths
before reloading their brains.

CONTENTS

Facts Don't Matter
to the Gun Ban Crowd

Gun control is an emotional issue, and the politics of gun control – the more accurate term would be gun prohibition – are steeped in emotionalism; often highly inflammatory rhetoric that demonizes firearms and the people who legally own them.

From deliberately misinterpreting and subsequently misrepresenting court rulings, to misquoting the Second Amendment and then fabricating arguments and making grossly exaggerated predictions, the anti-gun-rights lobby has turned the process of firearms demonization into an art form.

Attacks on gun rights come in many forms and they are not always overt. Often times they are purposefully subtle. Many veteran gun rights activists are familiar with the way Dennis Henigan, an attorney and vice president of the anti-gun Brady Campaign to Prevent Gun Violence, carefully misquoted the Second Amendment during an interview that has become a popular staple on YouTube. This was prior to the U.S. Supreme Court's landmark ruling in *District of Columbia v. Dick Anthony Heller* in June 2008, in which the high court ruled in a 5-4 decision with Justice Antonin Scalia writing for the majority that the Second Amendment protected and affirmed an individual civil right to keep and bear arms that extends well beyond service in a militia.

In discussing the Second Amendment, Henigan cleverly, and many believe *deliberately*, left out three key words. He quoted the Amendment as: "A well-regulated militia, being necessary to the security of a free state, the right to keep and bear arms shall not be infringed."

What's missing? The actual language of the Second Amendment reads: "A well regulated Militia, being necessary to the security of a free State, the right *of the people* to keep and bear Arms, shall not be infringed."

At the time, and even in the wake of the court's *Heller* ruling, gun prohibition advocates maintained the court had "re-written history" and refuted the long-maintained belief of gun banners that the right to keep and bear arms was something of a communal right. That is, they believed in what is typically referred to as "the collectivist view" that the Second Amendment only protected a state's right to organize and arm a militia.

This belief was largely founded on a misinterpretation – which many believe ultimately became a deliberate misrepresentation – of the high court's 1939 ruling in *U.S. v. Miller*, which went against a couple of bootleggers who had been convicted of, among other things, having a sawed-off shotgun. In his losing opinion on *Heller*, former Associate Justice John Paul Stevens, perhaps the court's most liberal justice, insisted that the *Miller* case established that the Second Amendment only protected a collective right, not an individual one. The argument had been made so often over the years that it became accepted as fact.

A careful reading of Justice Scalia's majority opinion, however, reveals that this argument is, and always has been, nonsense.

Here is what Justice Scalia wrote:

> *JUSTICE STEVENS places overwhelming reliance upon this Court's decision in United States v. Miller, 307 U. S. 174 (1939). "[H]undreds of judges," we are told, "have relied on the view of*

the amendment we endorsed there," post, at 2, and "[e]ven if the textual and historical arguments on both side of the issue were evenly balanced, respect for the well-settled views of all of our predecessors on this Court, and for the rule of law itself . . . would prevent most jurists from endorsing such a dramatic upheaval in the law," post, at 4. And what is, according to JUSTICE STEVENS, the holding of Miller that demands such obeisance? That the Second Amendment "protects the right to keep and bear arms for certain military purposes, but that it does not curtail the legislature's power to regulate the nonmilitary use and ownership of weapons."

Nothing so clearly demonstrates the weakness of JUSTICE STEVENS' case. Miller did not hold that and cannot possibly be read to have held that. The judgment in the case upheld against a Second Amendment challenge two men's federal convictions for transporting an unregistered short-barreled shotgun in interstate commerce, in violation of the National Firearms Act, 48 Stat. 1236. It is entirely clear that the Court's basis for saying that the Second Amendment did not apply was not that the defendants were "bear[ing] arms" not "for . . . military purposes" but for "nonmilitary use," post, at 2. Rather, it was that the type of weapon at issue was not eligible for Second Amendment protection: "In the absence of any evidence tending to show that the possession or use of a [shortbarreled shotgun] at this time has some reasonable relationship to the preservation or efficiency of a well regulated militia, we cannot say that the Second Amendment guarantees the right to keep and bear such an instrument." 307 U. S., at 178 (emphasis added). "Certainly," the Court continued, "it is not within judicial notice that this weapon is any part of the ordinary military equipment or that its use could contribute to the common defense." Ibid. Beyond that, the opinion provided no explanation of the content of the right.

This holding is not only consistent with, but positively suggests, that the Second Amendment confers an individual right to keep and bear arms (though only arms that "have some reasonable relationship to the preservation or efficiency of a well regulated militia"). Had the Court believed that the Second Amendment protects only those serving in the militia, it would have been odd to examine the character of the weapon rather than simply note that the two crooks were not militiamen. JUSTICE STEVENS can say again and again that Miller did "not turn on the difference between muskets and sawed-off shotguns, it turned, rather, on the basic difference between the military and nonmilitary use and possession of guns," post, at 42–43, but the words of the opinion prove otherwise. The most JUSTICE STEVENS can plausibly claim for Miller is that it declined to decide the nature of the Second Amendment right, despite the Solicitor General's argument (made in the alternative) that the right was collective, see Brief for United States, O. T. 1938, No. 696, pp. 4–5. Miller stands only for the proposition that the Second Amendment right, whatever its nature, extends only to certain types of weapons.

It is particularly wrongheaded to read Miller for more than what it said, because the case did not even purport to be a thorough examination of the Second Amendment.

JUSTICE STEVENS claims, post, at 42, that the opinion reached its conclusion "[a]fter reviewing many of the same sources that are discussed at greater length by the Court today."

Despite Justice Scalia's exhaustively researched opinion, which explored the history of the Second

Amendment, gun prohibitionists continued to argue that the *Heller* ruling was wrong, until they hit on another strategy. They determined that the ruling did allow for "reasonable regulation" of firearms, and then set about defining what, in their opinion, is "reasonable."

A careful look at some of the laws defended by the gun prohibition lobby clearly demonstrates that even local gun bans are "reasonable" in their opinion. The anti-gun community furiously defended the Chicago handgun ban that was essentially nullified by the Supreme Court majority in *McDonald v. City of Chicago* in June 2010. Prior to that, they argued just as strenuously in favor of continuing the District of Columbia ban that was struck down in the *Heller* ruling.

Likewise, they have supported one-gun-a-month limitation laws, and local ordinances and/or state laws prohibiting carrying firearms in certain places, bans on modern semiautomatic sporting rifles, more restrictive licensing and registration; all designed not only to make it more difficult to own firearms, but more importantly to also discourage citizens from even wanting to own them.

Naturally, in the gun prohibitionist lexicon, all such laws are "reasonable" and "sensible," both words carefully chosen to make it appear that any opposition to such infringements is both unreasonable and senseless.

It has not been credibly demonstrated that any of the restrictive gun control measures supported by the prohibitionist lobby have been effective in reducing crime. After the handgun ban was imposed in Washington, D.C. the homicide and violent crime rates skyrocketed. After the handgun ban was adopted in Chicago, the murder rate went way up. Data is abundantly available on the crime rates in both communities before and after bans were imposed. There is also data available that shows that in the first year following the Supreme Court's *Heller* ruling overturning the prohibition, violent crime dropped significantly in the District of Columbia.

Another favorite target of gun banners is the gun show. Prohibitionists have tried for years to demonize gun shows as "arms bazaars for criminals" and in the wake of the 9/11 terrorist attacks, the phrase was updated to "arms bazaars for criminals and terrorists." However, as noted by the National Rifle Association and other organizations, the anti-gun show rhetoric largely consists of myth.

For example, says the NRA, there is no such thing as an "unlicensed dealer" at a gun show. Licensed dealers may do business at gun shows, but private transactions between two individuals do not require a federal firearms license, except in cases where state statute – such as in California – requires all firearm transactions to be conducted through dealers for the purpose of subjecting each buyer to a background check.

This is the so-called "gun show loophole" that anti-gunners complain about, yet a string of studies by the FBI and Bureau of Justice Statistics (BJS) have consistently shown that a very tiny minority of criminals get their firearms from gun shows.

The NRA notes on its website that, "A 2006 FBI study of criminals who attacked law enforcement officers found that within their sample, "None of the [attackers'] rifles, shotguns, or handguns … were obtained from gun shows or related activities." Ninety-seven percent of guns in the study were obtained illegally, and the assailants interviewed had nothing but contempt for gun laws. As one offender put it, "[T]he 8,000 new gun laws would have made absolutely [no difference], whatsoever, about me getting a gun. … I never went into a gun store or to a gun show or to a pawn shop or anyplace else where firearms are legally bought and sold."

An earlier BJS report on Firearms Use by Offenders used information from surveys with 18,000 inmates at state prisons. This research revealed that less than one percent (0.7%) of guns used by criminals came from gun shows. Another BJS study, also mentioned on the NRA website, said that between 1992 and 1998, only 1.7 percent of federal prisoners got their firearms from gun shows.

This does not matter to the gun prohibition lobby because they see a gun show crackdown as a piece of trophy legislation, a prize. To pass legislation that ratchets down on gun show operations and perhaps puts some of them out of business would be a major political coup for a movement that has lost significant credibility and relevancy since the mid-term election in 1994 that saw more than 50 anti-gun Democrats lose their seats on Capitol Hill after the Clinton administration had pushed through a ten-year semi-auto ban and the Brady Law requiring federal background checks on gun purchases.

Closing the so-called "gun show loophole" – which actually translates to closing gun shows – is just one goal of the gun prohibition lobby. Many in the anti-gun camp demonize modern semiautomatic sporting rifles, also known as sport-utility rifles, as "assault weapons," even though the technically correct definition of an assault rifle applies only to *selective fire* weapons. A selective fire weapon is one that can be fired one round at a time, with a single press of the trigger, or switched to fire either fully automatic, with multiple rounds being fired with a single trigger press, or a three-shot burst with a single press on the trigger. They are not simply military-style looking rifles with certain cosmetic similarities to an actual military firearm.

Astonishingly, when once discussing via e-mail the difference with a reporter for an online daily newspaper in the Pacific Northwest, the reporter advised one of the authors that the term "assault weapon" had become so publicly acceptable that he would continue alluding to semi-auto military look-alikes as "assault weapons" because it is the norm. Succumbing to widespread public ignorance and one's own laziness is hardly a sterling example to set, but that illustrates the dilemma faced by firearms owners who have been demonized by a hostile press that has been all-too-accommodating to the gun prohibition lobby.

It is that mindset that has enabled gun prohibitionists to perpetuate myths and distortions to the point that they become accepted as fact by a large segment of the public that has changed over the course of one or two generations; a society raised by single parents – usually mothers – and estranged from their fathers; a society disconnected from its roots of self-reliance and self-determination that has become an urban society of entitlements and no motivation.

But as Abraham Lincoln once famously observed, "You can fool some of the people all of the time, and all of the people some of the time, but you can't fool all of the people all of the time."

America is not completely a land of fools, although some certainly reside here and it might be said that a few even occupy high public office. But their numbers appear to be shrinking, at least so far as the question of firearms civil rights is concerned.

This is why the gun prohibition movement that was once like a juggernaut has lost momentum and relevancy, though it could rise again under the right circumstances. A great many people have stopped being fooled though and they have started to realize that the anti-gun-rights lobby has essentially been shooting blanks. Arguments they presented against gun ownership and personal liberty have been unable to stand the test of time and careful scrutiny.

This did not happen overnight. It has taken hard work, dedication and a considerable investment of time, money and scholarly research. The benefit has been realized in court rulings and the re-emergence of individual's firearms freedoms.

But the battle will continue so long as there are self-appointed social "progressives" who deem it their mission to remove personally-owned firearms from society, and build their efforts on misperceptions, misrepresentations and outright fabrications because their desired end has justified whatever means they choose to accomplish their goals.

One

THERE WILL BE BLOOD IN THE STREETS

Q. *Why should a civilized society tolerate widespread private firearms ownership and the carrying of weapons? Won't that lead to more danger in our neighborhoods and more violent crime?*

During the late 1980s and early 1990s, America witnessed a tidal wave of legislation that enacted concealed carry statutes, imposed statewide authority for firearms regulation – leaving that authority in the hands of the various legislatures – and in a few cases, reforming older laws that had placed considerable discretionary authority in the hands of local police chiefs, sheriffs and judges on who, and more importantly who would not, receive a license to carry.

During debate on virtually all of these bills, regardless of the state, opponents of such legislation, typically led by a spokesman or spokeswoman from the local "CeaseFire" and/or "Million Mom March" chapter, offered dire warnings about what would happen as a result of passage. In simple terms, the message was uniformly repetitive: "There will be blood in the streets."

Arguments included increased danger to police officers and the public. There were predictions of gun battles resulting from heated tempers over fender-bender car accidents, mayhem at street intersections, and shootings in barrooms and taverns would erupt. And of course the gun prohibition lobby was always quick to contend that these laws would make it unsafe for children, without ever explaining how.

As alarmist rhetoric goes, it was admittedly first rate, depending upon the eloquence of the speaker. However, after the first dozen or so such debates were held across the country in different legislative forums, it became clear that all of these gun rights opponents appeared to be taking their talking points from the same gun control playbook. There was a pattern to the opposition, a repetition of arguments that almost invariably included not just the same broad predictions, but frequently used the very same words or phrases from one venue to the next.

Perhaps what anti-gun-rights zealots hadn't counted on was that academia would produce clear-thinking people like Professor John Lott to challenge them. Lott is the author of *More Guns = Less Crime*, which was in its third edition at this writing. The exhaustive book details crime patterns and how they relate to gun ownership and the availability of carry licenses.

The Violence Policy Center, a more extremist gun prohibition organization than the Brady Campaign to Prevent Gun Violence, has a website link called "Concealed Carry Killers," containing short news reports about people who use their concealed carry handgun to allegedly commit a crime. VPC keeps a running count of people with carry licenses and permits who perform a criminal act.

But there is one gargantuan hole in their logic, and it is in the realm of simple mathematics and percentages. At the time of this writing, there were fewer than 150 incidents in which 202 individuals reportedly lost their lives. Presented like that, it is an outrageous figure, tending to support everything that anti-gunners were claiming.

Not so fast with the conclusion, says Lott, who puts the argument in its proper perspective. These 122 incidents represent a miniscule fraction of the number of private citizens – at this writing more than six *million* people – who were licensed to carry. What you have in reality amounts to a tiny fraction of one percent of people who have gun permits who commit crimes.

Yet VPC Legislative Director Kristen Rand is content to raise eyebrows stating, "Contrary to the false assurances of concealed carry proponents, too many of those with valid permits kill in anger, not in self-defense."

It is essentially a ploy; an argument that has very little sound basis but appeals to some people on an emotional level by demonizing the broad and diverse self-defense community. Instead of simply acknowledging that a small number of people abuse their carry right, Rand and her gun prohibitionist contemporaries instead resort to rhetoric carefully designed to make citizens fearful of other citizens who carry defensive firearms.

Says Rand, "A permit to carry a concealed handgun has become one more weapon in the arsenal of domestic abusers who ultimately kill their intimate partner or other family member."

So, in her world, armed citizens become domestic thugs waiting to become killers. This rhetoric is aimed specifically at women, ideally causing them to become fearful of their male companions or spouses in the event they own or wish to purchase a firearm.

Remember this statistic: 122 incidents in 27 states, resulting in 202 fatalities.

Enter Lott, who notes that in the State of Florida alone, between Oct. 1, 1987 and May 21, 2010, "permits had been issued to 1.8 million people. On average, the permits had been held for quite a long time, well over 10 years. For all those individuals across the more than 22 years of legal carry, there were only 167 cases where the permit was revoked for a firearms related violation, or about *0.01 percent* of permit holders. While the state doesn't provide a precise breakdown of the reason for those revocations, the vast majority were apparently for people who accidentally carried their concealed handgun into a gun-free zone, such as an airport or school."

In an essay headlined "Gun Control Advocates Make Up Facts about Concealed Handgun Laws," Lott observed, "The Brady Campaign and the Violence Policy Center evaluate the benefits of concealed handgun laws based solely on the claimed costs — they don't compare the cases where defensive uses occurred to the bad things that happen, but only count what they claim are the bad cases. They ignore lots of amazing defensive gun use cases. But even more bizarrely, they count legitimate self-defense cases as bad events even when no charges are filed or the permit holder is later exonerated."

Lott noted that Florida is not alone when it comes to good behavior by its legally armed citizens. In Arizona, where there were more than 99,300 active carry permits as of December 1, 2007 there had been only 33 revocations during that year for any reason, which amounts to a 0.03 percent rate. In Texas, more than 208,900 citizens were legally licensed and a mere 160 were prosecuted and convicted of crimes ranging from misdemeanors to felonies, Lott added. That's a revocation rate of 0.05 percent, hardly a figure that should create widespread fear for the public safety.

Anti-gun hysteria does not limit itself to press releases and questionable "reports" from gun prohibition lobbying organizations. It has also seeped into the news and editorial columns of daily newspapers.

In an editorial opposing adoption of a "stand your ground" statute in Pennsylvania, the *Philadelphia Inquirer's* portrayed the proposed law as being one that would "expand gun owners' rights to blast away at anyone if they feel threatened outside their home or even in their car." Headlined "Misfire," went on to claim that "Even a front-porch encounter between an armed homeowner and a persistent door-to-door solicitor could see lead fly."

This sort of alarmist forecasting has only served, over time, to erode the credibility of the gun control movement. Time is the enemy of all social campaigns because time is the one factor that either proves or disproves all of the espoused theories and predictions. That has certainly been the case with gun control.

Opponents of individual firearms ownership had at one time enjoyed considerable public support and people unquestioningly believed their forecasts of widespread trouble and even carnage with expanded gun ownership. However, time passed and with it passed the credibility of the gun control lobby.

About midway in 2010, the FBI released crime data that, for a third consecutive year, showed violent crime had fallen in the United States. That was encouraging news for everyone but the gun prohibition lobby, because the decline in crime coincided with a period of increased gun sales, many of them to first-time buyers.

Reacting to the news, coauthor Alan Gottlieb, who is also chairman of the Citizens Committee for the Right to Keep and Bear Arms, a grassroots lobbying and activist organization, said the continuing trend proves that gun control lobby rhetoric has been "consistently and demonstrably wrong."

"No matter how gun prohibitionists try to spin this," Gottlieb said, "the bottom line is that they have been consistently and demonstrably wrong, and they know it. On the other hand, gun rights organizations have been consistently right when we argued that increased gun ownership would not lead to higher crime rates, and might even have a deterrent effect, because even property crimes are down, according to this year's report."

The National Shooting Sports Foundation noted that "The FBI statistics undermine a favorite argument of anti-gun groups and some mainstream media that 'more guns equal more crime,' especially when you consider that the decrease in violent crime in 2009 occurred at the same time that firearm sales were surging."

According to the FBI report, murder declined 7.3 percent in 2009, robberies fell 8 percent, aggravated assault dropped by 4.2 percent and forcible rape declined 2.6 percent from 2008 figures.

"What the data tells us is exactly the opposite of what the gun ban lobby has predicted for several years," Gottlieb observed. "Their dire predictions that America's streets would run red have been shown up as a fraudulent sales pitch for public disarmament."

Highlights of the FBI report included:

• Each of the violent crime categories decreased from 2008—murder (7.3 percent), robbery (8.0 percent), aggravated assault (4.2 percent), and forcible rape (2.6 percent).
• Each of the property crime categories also dropped from 2008—motor vehicle theft (17.1 percent), larceny-theft (4.0 percent), and burglary (1.3 percent).
• Among the 1,318,398 violent crimes were 15,241 murders; 88,097 forcible rapes; 408,217 robberies; and 806,843 aggravated assaults.
• Among the 9,320,971 property crimes were an estimated 2,199,125 burglaries; 6,327,230 larceny-thefts; 794,616 thefts of motor vehicles; and 58,871 arsons.
• During 2009, the South accounted for 42.5 percent of all violent crime in the nation, followed by the West (22.9 percent), the Midwest (19.6 percent), and the Northeast (15.0 percent).
• During 2009, 43.9 percent of all property crimes in the U.S. were recorded in the South, with 22.7 percent in the West, 20.8 percent in the Midwest, and 12.6 percent in the Northeast.
• In 2009, agencies nationwide made about 13.7 million arrests, excluding traffic violations. Of those arrests, an estimated 581,765 were for violent crimes.
• Nearly 75 percent of all arrested persons in the nation during 2009 were male. Slightly more than 77 percent of all murder victims were also male.
• Firearms were used in 67.1 percent of the nation's murders, along with 42.6 percent of robberies and 20.9 percent of aggravated assaults. (Weapons data is not collected for forcible rapes.)

• Collectively, victims of property crimes (excluding arson) lost an estimated $15.2 billion during 2009.

Anecdotal evidence from various states indicated that more citizens had obtained carry licenses and permits. Some estimates, including one from Lott made during a presentation at the 2010 Gun Rights Policy Conference held in San Francisco, California, placed the number of legally-licensed-to-carry gun owners at about 6.2 million, and that figure did not take into account the number of citizens in Arizona, Alaska and Vermont who carry without a permit because those states do not actually require a permit. This figure may be even higher today.

Additionally, there has been a growing open carry movement that may account for tens of thousands more armed citizens. These individuals, acting within state constitutional or statutory guidelines, routinely carry their defensive handguns in the open. This has created something of an educational challenge relating to the public and local law enforcement agencies, but in state after state where the necessary research has been conducted by attorneys general or city attorneys, they have concluded that there are no laws prohibiting open carry. Simply because the practice went out of vogue well into the last century does not mean it was made illegal.

Data for the FBI crime report came from city, county, state, tribal, federal, university and college agencies that participated in the Uniform Crime Reporting program in 2009. These agencies, according to the FBI, represent 96.3 percent of the nation's population.

Such revelations amount to damning indictments of the gun prohibition movement, and its contention that large numbers of firearms in private hands could have no other logical effect than increased homicides and assaults that did not result in deaths. But the data has said otherwise.

One thing about gun prohibitionists is that they will not allow a public setback to get in their way. When they have had to fall back, they inevitably return to arguments that have given them traction in the past, and hopefully will deflect public attention from the story that is causing them their momentary embarrassment. At the same time, they turn their attention in a different direction. They may attack gun shows, or lack of waiting periods, and ever since the Supreme Court's ruling in *District of Columbia v. Dick Anthony Heller*, which suggested that some forms of firearms regulation may be constitutional, they have been pushing for "reasonable gun regulations" they claim the *Heller* ruling will allow. They have yet to define what constitutes a "reasonable regulation," but prior to the *Heller* ruling and the subsequent ruling in *McDonald v. City of Chicago*, gun prohibition groups felt that total handgun bans in both Chicago and the District of Columbia were "reasonable."

It is astonishingly callous how quickly the gun prohibitionist lobby will push its agenda even when a specific situation may have nothing to do with that agenda.

A text book example occurred in March 2006 in Seattle, Washington. Several young people were killed by a lone perpetrator in a house located in Seattle's Capitol Hill neighborhood. The gunman, Kyle Aaron Huff, subsequently took his own life when an armed police officer approached the shooting scene.

Subsequently, the state's anti-gun lobbying organization, Washington CeaseFire, teamed up with then-Seattle Mayor Greg Nickels to demand legislation that would have, among other things, added strict regulations to gun show operations.

Huff did not get any of his firearms from a gun show. There is no evidence he ever attended a gun show. The firearms he used were ones that he brought to Seattle when he moved there from Montana. He had purchased the guns there from a retail gun shop.

Indeed, none of the measures proposed by gun prohibitionists in the wake of the "Capitol Hill Massacre" would have prevented Huff from committing the crime. They would have had no deterrent effect at all.

Groups like CeaseFire and the Brady Campaign to Prevent Gun Violence would like to see more restrictions placed on the issuance of concealed carry licenses and permits. They cite shootings that occur in bars or outside late-night clubs, and shootings that involve juvenile gang bangers.

What they conveniently overlook are some revealing facts. The overwhelming majority of those nightclub shootings involve perpetrators who do not have concealed carry permits, and in many cases, they would not qualify for such a permit because they have criminal records or they are under the required age to be carrying a firearm. Frequently, the firearms they use are stolen or obtained from family members or street acquaintances.

Likewise, when juvenile gunmen are involved in such an incident, the gun ban lobby completely ignores the fact that concealed carry permits are not available to juveniles – people under the age of 18 – anywhere in the United States. In most states, the minimum age to obtain a carry permit is 21. We are talking about young thugs and gang wannabes; people in their mid-to late-teens, primarily, who are involved in far too many of these incidents. All of these juvenile shooters are carrying guns illegally, but instead of tackling that issue head-on, gun prohibitionists deflect the argument and go after the carry licenses of law-abiding *adults*.

It is not that they necessarily believe that placing restrictions on legally-armed adults will somehow result in a lower violent crime rate among juveniles, but it *is* important that they want *you* to believe it.

The public should ask why, since the mainstream press has done such a woefully inadequate job of questioning gun prohibitionists and their motives.

Perhaps the key to this is what Joe Waldron, a retired Marine Lieutenant Colonel and legislative director of the Citizens Committee for the Right to Keep and Bear Arms, has repeatedly observed about the term "gun control."

"The operative word is 'control'," Waldron says unabashedly.

In the philosophical view of gun prohibitionists, a "civilized society" is one in which there are few, if any legally-owned private firearms, and those would be strictly regulated.

This is why the anti-gun Brady Campaign and state affiliates such as Washington CeaseFire were aghast when legally-armed citizens – and especially those who consider themselves open carry activists and advocates – are not routinely barred from coffee shops and other public areas in states where open carry is legal and even constitutionally protected. To see a private citizen, or group of citizens, casually gathering for coffee or dinner, while openly carrying defensive firearms, is a culture shock to people who are not accustomed to seeing firearms carried by anyone but uniformed police officers.

Early in 2010, the Brady Campaign and other anti-gunners attempted to browbeat the Seattle-based Starbucks Coffee Company from allowing open carry practitioners in their stores. Starbucks' response was business-like and matter-of-fact: The company will follow and recognize state and local gun laws and ordinances and its doors are open to all of their loyal customers. There had not been a single incident of unruliness or dangerous behavior by any open carrier, yet gun prohibitionists wanted them banned, claiming that their presence somehow made Starbucks shops unsafe for families.

It quickly became obvious that the Brady Campaign wanted Starbucks to become something of a commercial surrogate in its attempt to foment hysteria and social bigotry against armed citizens. After all, the Brady group had been successful in California in its efforts to pressure other restaurants and coffee shops to ban open carriers, but when they tried the same tactic with Starbucks, their campaign hit the proverbial brick wall.

The result of this attempted boycott by the anti-gun lobby may have been a classic backfire. As reported on the financial pages of several newspapers, six months after the Starbucks flap, Starbucks reported that its earnings had risen for the third quarter of 2010, to a whopping $278.9 million, which translated to 37 cents per share. That was up significantly compared to the third quarter of 2009, when Starbucks reported earnings of $150 million, or 20 cents a share.

Chicken Little predictions from the Brady Campaign that the financial sky would fall on Starbucks turned out to be wishful thinking at best. When the gun prohibitionists went after Starbucks, the firearms community – especially the Open Carry activists who were the principle target of the Brady camp's social bigotry – increased their patronage at the coffee giant's shops. While that would hardly account for more than $100 million in additional profit – and it would be nonsense to even suggest that possibility – the fact that these openly-armed citizens, and others who carried their guns concealed, brought their business to Starbucks quite obviously did not frighten other customers away. It would be ludicrous to suggest that nobody knew armed patrons were supporting Starbucks with their business because the effort gained national media attention. In the process, not a single Starbucks customer came to any harm at the hands of one of these legally-armed private citizens.

It was no surprise that not a peep was heard from the gun control crowd when Starbucks announced its spike in earnings. It was coffee that flowed freely at Starbucks, not the blood of its customers. The attempt to intimidate Starbucks not only sputtered into oblivion, it may have actually driven more paying customers to the company's coffee shops.

In his essay, Prof. Lott mentioned that anti-gunners habitually only tell one side of the story. They never mention successful self-defense uses of handguns, even though there is an abundance of evidence that armed citizens have interrupted and prevented violent crimes and saved innocent victims in the process. The authors detailed this side of the story in our book, *America Fights Back: Armed Self-Defense in a Violent Age*. The book contained dozens of reports about armed citizens who successfully defended themselves and their loved ones, and occasionally total strangers, from violent criminal attack.

Mike Stuckey, senior news editor for MSNBC.COM in early 2010, detailed one such account that was hardly atypical of a self-defense gun use by an armed private citizen. South Carolina attorney Jim Corley was one of four people in a meeting hall in April 2009 when an armed thug burst into the building, located in the Five Points neighborhood of Columbia.

When 18-year-old gunman Kayson Helms yelled to the group to "Gimme what you got!" he committed what renowned self-defense authority Massad Ayoob, founder of the Lethal Force Institute, has termed "a fatal error in the victim selection process." Attorney Corley was only too obliging, reaching into his hip pocket, where he had a .32-caliber Kel Tec pistol in a pocket holster.

The attorney's first shot hit Helms in the abdomen. His second and third rounds struck the robber in the neck and torso. According to Stuckey's report, Helms managed to run but he did not get far. Authorities found him dead about 100 feet from the robbery scene.

This was not the oft-predicted public mayhem that the gun prohibition lobby had forecast with passage of a concealed carry statute, but the lawful use of a firearm under the parameters of the state's self-defense code; i.e. the intended use of a piece of emergency survival equipment.

It should be noted that Helms did not carry his gun legally at all. He was not legally armed under South Carolina's statute, but armed in spite of the law. That he died at such a young age is certainly no cause for joy, but it must be kept in perspective that Helms and only Helms set the stage for his final moments. Nobody forced him to attempt an armed robbery that ultimately ended with his death at the hands of one of his intended victims.

In his report, Stuckey accurately noted, "Statistics from the national Centers for Disease Control do indicate that the murder and mayhem predicted by many opponents of concealed-carry laws have not come to pass."

He also quoted Jim Kessler from the Third Way, a liberal think tank that began life as Americans for Gun Safety, who acknowledged that he had not seen "any evidence...that (concealed carry) creates havoc."

Yet, gun prohibitionists simply refuse to budge. Kristen Rand, VPC spokeswoman, admitted to Stuckey that "We don't have centralized data-gathering to know what people are doing with" concealed carry licenses. But she quickly insisted that "anecdotally, we know they're doing quite a bit of harm."

As evidence, the VPC uses its website to highlight the crimes committed by a relative handful of people with carry permits, as noted earlier in this chapter. Again, one merely needs to do some basic math to figure out that less than 150 reported crimes does not stack up at all when taken as some sort of representation of the behavior of more than 6.2 million legally-licensed citizens. The argument simply does not pass the proverbial smell test. For every "anecdote" about the misuse of a defensive firearm by some licensed gun owner, there are dozens, perhaps scores of documented cases when the intervention or mere presence of an armed citizen saved lives.

In the final analysis, irrefutable facts get in the way of questionable rhetoric. Violent crime rates declined during a period of increased gun ownership and expansion of concealed carry laws, and the rise of the Open Carry movement.

Perhaps historians will one day observe that it was not nearly so much blood that flowed as did the bull.

Two

BANNING GUNS MAKES SOCIETY SAFER

Q. *If we remove all firearms from private hands, won't that make our neighborhoods safer for families?*

Considerable disagreement exists about the value of gun control as an effective crime prevention tool in the United States, and certainly among gun prohibitionists the data can be spun to suggest that gun bans – such as the ban on so-called "assault weapons" under the Clinton administration in the 1990s – have reduced violent crime.

However, there is also data that refutes such claims; data that cannot be simply dismissed as anecdotal.

An anti-gun-rights website, guninformation.org, has branded as a myth the fact that the crime rate skyrocketed in Great Britain following the enactment of strict gun laws. They made this claim by arguing that British police had changed their system for recording crime, which made it "appear that the crime rate went up." This argument is provided typically to rebut gun control critics in the United States.

However, the *London Daily Mail* has reported repeatedly that gun crime nearly doubled in England and

Wales under Labour party control. The newspaper also reported that in some parts of the country, where handgun ownership was essentially outlawed following the March 1996 Dunblane Massacre, "the number of offences has increased more than five-fold."

Of course, much of the violence, according to the newspaper, was linked to gang activity, but so it is in the United States as well.

Arguing that the rise in crime may be a statistical illusion is an argument that only goes so far. Renowned firearms researcher John Lott, writing as a senior research scientist at the University of Maryland at the time, noted in an article that appeared in the *Philadelphia Inquirer* that there is no evidence that banning guns cuts crime.

At the time, in Spring 2008, Lott had the benefit of being able to study data from the "assault weapons" ban years from 1994-2004. Reacting to a proposal in Philadelphia to restore the ban as a reaction to violent crime wave, Lott reminded readers in the "City of Brotherly Love" – which had recorded 406 homicides in 2007 – that "all the published academic studies by criminologists and economists find that neither the initial ban in 1994 nor its sun-setting in 2004 changed rates of murder or other violent crimes."

"Similarly," he added, "there is no evidence that state bans have mattered."

Prof. Lott has what gun prohibitionists consider an annoying habit of explaining the obvious from the perspective of a scientific researcher, rather than someone who can be merely pigeon-holed as a gun advocate or a crank. He is an economist, not a gun aficionado.

In the same article, Lott told readers that "the U.S. murder rate was 5.7 per 100,000 people in 2003, the last full year before the law sunset. It was still 5.7 in 2006."

"Over the same period," he observed, "the rate of violent crimes fell slightly. In the 43 states without their own assault-weapons bans, the murder rates fell, while they rose in the seven states with such bans. Violent-crime rates fell more quickly in the 43 without bans than in the seven states with them.

"Yet it always seems easier," Lott continued, "for politicians to blame the lack of gun control rather than focusing on their own responsibilities. When Washington and Chicago experienced explosions in murder and violent crime after banning handguns, leaders there did not blame their bans, but rather they blamed the rest of the country that had not also adopted stricter regulations."

He asked readers whether it was "really surprising that Philadelphia's murder rates have risen while its arrest rates have fallen?"

In an article he wrote about the Chicago case just before the Supreme Court handed down its historic ruling in *McDonald v. City of Chicago* – the Second Amendment Foundation's case against the city that has frequently been erroneously confused with the National Rifle Association's case against the city – Prof. Lott drove home the point about the effect of gun bans on Chicago and Washington, D.C.

"Murder rates soared in D.C. and Chicago after their gun bans were put in place. As shown in the just released third edition of my book *More Guns, Less Crime*, before the late-1982 ban, Chicago's murder rate was falling relative to those in the nine other largest cities, the 50 largest cities, the five counties that border Cook County (in which the city is located), and the U.S. as a whole. After the ban, Chicago's murder rate rose relative to all these other places. Compared with the 50 most populous cities, Chicago's murder rate went from equaling the average for the other cities in 1982, to exceeding their average murder rate by 32 percent in 1992, to exceeding their average by 68 percent in 2002."

Gun prohibitionists seem to linger in a world apart from the rest of us, believing in the sudden arrival of some kind of Utopian existence if we merely gave up the means of self-defense. There would be no crime or violence because there are no firearms, no means of physical conflict. This may be one reason why they are so consistently and adamantly opposed to passage of so-called "castle doctrine" statutes, which are, in reality, "stand-your-ground" laws that allow a private citizen the right to defend himself if attacked in any place where he has a right to be, such as a public venue that might include a shopping mall, parking lot, theater, grocery store or a public sidewalk. These laws allow the citizen to "stand his ground" rather than demonstrate that prior to using force in self-defense, an effort was made to retreat.

A growing number of people, including most self-defense experts, disdain the "duty to retreat" requirements in some states, arguing that they essentially give an attacker a clear shot at your back as you flee.

The argument was presented by Matthew Major, opinion editor and member of the *Public Opinion* editorial board in Pennsylvania that "stand-your-ground" laws are not necessary. In his words, they "attempt to fix what isn't broken."

"After all," he contended, "it only stands to reason that removing the need to retreat when confronted with a possible threat will result in more guns a-blazing, knives a-stabbing and cudgels a-swinging.

"Maybe, in such cases, lives would be saved," Major continued. "But it's just as likely mistakes will be made, and the innocent will suffer."

This is the same general argument posited by self-defense opponents all over the map when such issues arise in the Legislature. "The innocent may suffer."

This may come as a surprise to Mr. Major and his contemporaries, but the innocent are already suffering, and have suffered, for generations. This is why the public has strongly supported concealed carry reform and state preemption statutes, and why the public is infuriated when people are prosecuted in the wake of cases in which they clearly acted in self-defense. While such prosecutions are becoming rarer, as prosecutors who run for election understand public sentiment, but they still happen.

Even in Chicago, prior to the 2010 Supreme Court ruling in the *McDonald* case, two rather high-profile self-defense cases involving private citizens, who used handguns that they illegally had in their homes under the existing ban at the time, were not prosecuted. In one case, a street thug named Anthony Nelson, whose street nickname was "Big Ant" and who had a 13-page rap sheet that included drug and weapons convictions dating back to 1998, made "a fatal error in the victim selection process."

Nelson was armed at the time on May 26, 2010 – a month before the high court ruling in *McDonald* – when he fired a shot at an elderly couple through their bedroom window in a West Side Chicago neighborhood. To his surprise, the intended male victim, an 80-year-old Korean War veteran, had his own handgun and he fired back at Nelson.

Nelson was fatally wounded but not too many tears outside of his immediate family were shed.

The overriding fatal flaw in any legislation that bans firearm ownership is that criminals will not abide by such a ban. "Big Ant" Nelson was a living testament to that simple, undeniable fact; because with his criminal record, he could not legally own, or even handle a firearm of any kind. Especially in Chicago, where handguns were banned at the time, Nelson could not legally ever have had that pistol.

Criminals, by their very nature, do not obey the law. For them, a ban on firearms has simply emboldened them to arm themselves and take advantage of a target rich environment, much like a pack of wolves would do in the presence of a flock of sheep where no shepherds or sheep dogs were present. To suggest that anyone who has made a life of crime would suddenly experience an epiphany and lay down his weapons if Congress or a state legislature enacted a ban on guns is ludicrous, if not downright delusional.

No greater testament to that fact could come from anywhere than it did from an editorial in the *Baltimore Sun*, a rabidly anti-gun-rights newspaper that recognized the dilemma possibly without realizing that they were acknowledging one of the firearms community's most basic arguments. In their editorial headlined "Armed and

Dangerous," the *Sun* editorial board noted, "Nearly half the people arrested and convicted in Baltimore City for violent crimes such as murder and armed robbery had previous convictions for handgun offenses. Yet the sentences they received for illegal gun possession didn't deter them. Many were back on the streets within a matter of weeks after being released, free to commit more mayhem." While this recidivism seems to surprise the *Sun's* editorial writers, it hardly surprises anyone who has made the decision to carry a defensive firearm for personal protection.

"The juvenile offender convicted of murdering former City Councilman Ken Harris in 2008, for example," the editorial lamented, "had served fewer than three months in jail for a handgun violation before he fatally shot Mr. Harris less than six weeks after his release. There are hundreds of cases where victims might still be alive if their killers had remained locked up."

This was certainly the motivation that guided the authors of the original "Three Strikes and You're Out" legislation in Washington State. The concept for the original measure came from the offices of the Second Amendment Foundation – the firearm civil rights organization that went on to win the landmark *McDonald v. City of Chicago* lawsuit 13 years later, mentioned earlier in this chapter.

Within the firearms community is the strong belief that neighborhoods are made safer not only by keeping criminals behind bars, but by the mere threat that some private citizen might be armed. Many gun rights activists are fond of suggesting to their anti-gun counterparts that if they strongly believe firearms are not a deterrent to crime, they should voluntarily post their residences with signs notifying all visitors, passers-by and potential robbers that "This is a gun-free home." It comes as no surprise when an avowed gun prohibitionist declines to post such signs.

In the years after Kennesaw, Georgia adopted an ordinance requiring heads of households to have a firearm – a move that was in direct reaction to the adoption of the handgun ban in Morton Grove, Illinois – the crime rate, small as it was, plummeted to virtually nil. The ordinance was essentially a social statement because it contains exemptions on several grounds, but publicity surrounding the adoption of that ordinance evidently had something of a deterrent effect on local burglars and other miscreants.

Earlier in this chapter, we alluded to the crime rate in Chicago and Washington, D.C. after both city governments imposed handgun bans. But what happened after the bans were lifted?

There is evidence at least from the District of Columbia, where the *Heller* ruling struck down the ban in 2008 that the violent crime rate went down. The *Washington Post* noted in a July 2009 article that the plummeting crime rate had perplexed experts.

The *Post* story noted, "Violent crime has plummeted in the Washington area and in major cities across the country, a trend criminologists describe as baffling and unexpected.

"The District, New York and Los Angeles are on track for fewer killings this year than in any other year in at least four decades. Boston, San Francisco, Minneapolis and other cities are also seeing notable reductions in homicides."

The newspaper quoted criminologist Andrew Karmen, a professor of sociology at the John Jay College of Criminal Justice in New York: "Experts did not see this coming at all."

"Criminologists have different theories about why crime is down so much," the *Washington Post* noted, "although many agree that the common belief that crime is connected to the economy is false."

Almost one year later, Prof. Lott – writing for FoxNews.com – had this to say:

"When the *Heller* decision was handed down in 2008 striking down Washington, D.C.'s handgun ban and gunlock regulations, Chicago's Mayor Richard Daley predicted disaster. He said that overturning the gun ban was 'a very frightening decision' and predicted more deaths along with Wild West-style shootouts and that people 'are going to take a gun and they are going to end their lives in a family dispute.' Washington's Mayor Adrian

Fenty similarly warned: 'More handguns in the District of Columbia will only lead to more handgun violence.'

"Yet, Armageddon never arrived."

Readers will note that this is the same "sky-is-falling" rhetoric discussed in the previous chapter. However, as Lott discovered with the benefit of time to observe the actual aftermath of the *Heller* ruling, the truth turned out to be quite different from the hysteria-laden prognostications of then Chicago and Washington, D.C. Mayors Richard Daley and Adrian Fenty.

"Washington's murder rate has plummeted -- falling by 25 percent in 2009 alone," Lott wrote. "This compares with a national drop of only 7 percent last year. And D.C.'s drop has continued this year.

"Comparing Washington's crime rates from January 1 to June 17 of (2010) to the same period in 2008," he continued, "shows a 34 percent drop in murder. This drop puts D.C.'s murder rate back to where it was before the 1977 handgun ban. Indeed, the murder rate is as low as was before 1967.

"Other gun crimes have also fallen in Washington," Lott noted. "While robberies without guns fell by 7 percent, robberies with guns fell by over 14 percent. Assaults with weapons other than guns fell by 7, but assaults using guns fell by over 20 percent."

Taking all of this information into consideration, while there has never been and probably could not be a single conclusive finding that increased gun ownership contributes to a reduction in crime, it does appear that there may be a correlation between high rates of gun ownership and lower rates of violent crime. This observation, even offered as a presumption, will no doubt elicit negative reactions ranging from sarcasm to accusations of scientific blasphemy. Yet, as Sir Arthur Conan Doyle observed through his fictional detective Sherlock Holmes, "When you have eliminated the impossible, whatever remains, however improbable, must be the truth."

One might reasonably inquire of all the experts who had been baffled about the drop in violent crime, particularly homicides, about why they did not "see it coming at all." It may be that academics fail, by social and philosophical conditioning, to recognize the genuine and perceived effectiveness of at least the threat of confrontation with an armed citizen. No recidivist worth his stolen goods will deny that he has more visceral fear of being shot by an intended victim than by an arresting police officer. They know that police want to bring them in to stand before a judge. Armed private citizens acting in self-defense have no such reflexive inclinations. They will often shoot, and even if the bullet wound is not fatal, it could leave the would-be criminal with a permanent or long-lasting disability that not simply ends his criminal career, but could put him at the mercy of street foes.

This logic may not be lost on self-defense experts or even on police, but it consistently eludes anti-gunners. Or, as is the more likely case, they simply ignore the possibility because it does not fit well with their preconceived notions of how best to assure public safety. Rather than acknowledge that they are deliberately ignoring one possible, and plausible, element of the puzzle because of a bias against private firearms ownership, these lofty researchers – the so-called "experts" – instead maintain what might be described as a perpetual state of at least partial denial.

In his waning days as governor of Pennsylvania, Democrat Ed Rendell – an avowed anti-gunner who had previously served as mayor of Philadelphia – vetoed legislation that would have ended a requirement under state law that people attacked outside of their own home must first make every effort to retreat before defending themselves. His justification for the veto was that he feared enabling would-be victims to stand their ground in the face of criminal attack might "encourage violent and deadly confrontations."

This reasoning left at least one Pennsylvania newspaper publisher openly wondering if Rendell was not on the side of the criminals. In a blistering editorial, *Jonestown Tribune-Democrat* publisher Robin L. Quillon wrote that "...for the past two terms, this governor has been hell-bent on chipping away at law-abiding citizens' right to protect themselves and their property."

There exists any number of anecdotal stories about how, following a natural disaster or during periods of civil unrest when emergency services such as police and fire are simply not available, armed residents have patrolled neighborhoods and kept looters or rioters out. Who can forget images of Asian shopkeepers standing on the roofs of their businesses in Los Angeles during the Rodney King riots, displaying and even firing weapons at oncoming crowds of violent demonstrators?

In the wake of Hurricane Katrina, some neighborhoods in the New Orleans area, particularly in Algiers, were patrolled by armed citizens because there literally was no available law enforcement to discourage looters. True, police had been dispatched to physically seize firearms from private citizens – an effort that quickly brought a successful federal lawsuit filed jointly by the Second Amendment Foundation and National Rifle Association – but they obviously didn't get all of the privately-held guns. For several days until some semblance of order was restored, it was up to the private citizen to fend for himself, and possibly his neighbors.

Yet it came as no great surprise when the anti-gun Brady Campaign to Prevent Gun Violence filed a brief opposing a lawsuit filed by the Second Amendment Foundation seeking to overturn North Carolina's Emergency Powers Act. That act gave the governor and local elected officials the authority to essentially suspend the Second Amendment during declared emergencies; that is, citizens would not be permitted to have firearms outside of their residences in the wake of a flood, hurricane or some other natural or man-made disaster, even when it is virtually assured that communications will be in chaos and help might not be coming.

Several states have such Emergency Powers statutes, but in the aftermath of the ruling by the U.S. Supreme Court in SAF's *McDonald v. City of Chicago* lawsuit challenging the city's handgun ban, the Second

Amendment is now incorporated to the states through the 14th Amendment, placing a limit on the kinds of things local and state governments can do in the realm of gun control, and a blanket prohibition on guns outside the home doe not appear to pass muster.

True to form for former Brady Campaign President Paul Helmke, when the court filing was announced, he issued a press release that tried to spin the lawsuit as an effort to promote anarchy. Helmke offered the rather incredulous argument that the Second Amendment "does not grant a right of vigilantes to take up arms on our streets during a riot or state of emergency."

National Gun Rights Examiner David Codrea, whose on-line gun rights blog reaches daily across cyberspace, was quick to react. In a blistering rebuttal, he reminded Helmke that the Second Amendment does not "grant" anything. Instead, the amendment merely affirms and protects a pre-existing right. Helmke would have people believe that it is acceptable to leave citizens defenseless in an emergency, when police will likely not be responding to 911 calls because there is no communications, perhaps roads are destroyed or flooded, and citizens are essentially on their own.

People who are left defenseless in such a doomsday scenario are literally at the non-existent mercy of any band of marauders that happens by. That is why, in the wake of Hurricane Katrina in 2005, the National Rifle Association and local affiliate organizations successfully lobbied in several states for the adoption of laws that prohibit government officials from ordering gun confiscations.

That makes even more sense today with a few years of available crime data that demonstrates expanded gun ownership has not resulted in an increase of violent crime. Data collected by the FBI for its annual crime report showed that in the years from 2007-2010 – a period that saw a dramatic increase in gun ownership and the number of people carrying concealed handguns.

As noted earlier in this chapter and in Chapter One, the impact of more guns and more carried guns did not result in the "blood-in-the-streets" predictions that seemed invariably to precede adoption of concealed carry statutes or so-called "Castle Doctrine" laws. Indeed, quite the opposite happened, and we noted earlier in this chapter how this perplexed the so-called "experts."

One region of the country where this phenomenon underscored the abject silliness of those Chicken Little predictions is Seattle, Washington. The city is something of a liberal cultural center in the midst of a state that is historically independent, but conservatively so. Seattle is similar in size to Washington, D.C. yet it enjoys one of the lowest homicide rates in the nation for a city with its population. During the first half of 2010, for example, the city recorded only seven criminal homicides.

In 2009, it had fewer than 25 homicides, and that number seems fairly consistent for the previous decade.

Washington State has one of the largest per capita numbers of legally-armed citizens of any state. At this writing, the state had some 270,000 concealed pistol licenses, and because it is an "open carry" state where citizens can legally carry a firearm openly, a lot of people have a lot of firearms. There is no mandatory gun registration, the right to bear arms is protected and delineated in the State Constitution. The farther one gets away from the I-5 corridor running from Vancouver on the Columbia River to Blaine at the Canadian border, the higher the percentage of armed households one will find. As one of the authors observed, get very far off the pavement and Washington can still be wild.

The FBI crime data showed that the nearby cities of Tacoma and Bellevue had even more impressive homicide statistics. Bellevue posted no homicides and Tacoma had only six, and that was up over the same period in 2009 when there were but four criminal homicides.

So, what happened to all of the predicted blood and gore? It never materialized.

Whether there will ever be a verifiable method of determining the positive impact of high regional gun ownership on the local crime data has not been studied because it is virtually impossible to keep track of all the crimes that were not committed because the intended victims, or their neighbors, had firearms.

What is evident, regardless of the knee-jerk dismissal of such a premise by the gun prohibition lobby, is that high rates of firearms ownership, especially coupled with a high percentage of legally-armed citizens carrying concealed or visible handguns, have not resulted in the grim scenarios predicted by gun rights opponents.

Are neighborhoods safer with or without firearms? Safety is not measured by data alone, but it is certainly a key component. One must keep in perspective that some people simply do not feel safe around firearms, even if the guns are owned by a neighbor who keeps them locked in a basement safe. But the presence of those firearms, and the potential for their use by the intended victim of a crime, may be the single most important factor in whether a criminal decides to visit your street, or someone else's.

You may not "feel" safe with a gun in the neighborhood, but just how safe might you be if criminals know there are no guns in the neighborhood?

Three

ONLY THE POLICE SHOULD HAVE GUNS

Q. *Why should anyone other than a sworn police officer carry a handgun?*

Rare is the moment in the United States or anywhere else that a policeman happens to be present at the scene of a crime, and as the authors noted in our earlier collaboration *America Fights Back: Armed Self-Defense in a Violent Age*, it is the armed citizen who frequently becomes the true "first responder" to a violent felony.

Almost reflexively, after a shooting in which an armed private citizen has intervened and prevented a dangerous crime from becoming deadly for the victims, local police officials caution the public against such intervention, even when it is clear that lives were saved. Whether one believes that the police are merely trying to keep citizens from being hurt, or they are acting to perpetuate the public impression that only the police can handle dangerous situations, the facts of such cases do tend to not support the notion that people are incapable of dealing with danger on their own.

We should first dispense with the obvious. A nation where only police have guns is a police state. Like it or not, such environments are breeding grounds for law enforcement abuse.

We will also put to rest a myth. The scenario imagined by gun prohibition advocates conveniently or ignorantly – or both — overlook what former Vice President Al Gore might call "an inconvenient truth." It is not only police who would have guns, no matter how hard the government envisioned by the gun ban lobby tries. Criminals would also have guns. They would never give them up willingly, and they would steal them from police if no other recourse was available.

For the moment, we will discuss the legitimate role of armed citizens in a free country.

Most people recall the horrible Oct. 16, 1991 massacre at the Luby's restaurant in Killeen, Texas. A madman named George Hennard drove a truck through the front of the restaurant, which was filled with patrons. He jumped out and opened fire with two handguns. He killed 23 people and wounded 20 others. Much of the damage was done by the time police arrived, confronted and engaged Hennard, and wounded him before he turned one of his guns on himself.

Contrast that mayhem with the incident two months later and two states away, the "massacre we didn't hear about" as described by J. Neil Schulman, took place at a Shoney's restaurant in Anniston, Alabama. On Dec. 17, two armed men came into the restaurant to rob the place, but then put everyone in a walk-in refrigerator and locked it.

Well, not everyone actually; a customer named Thomas Glenn Terry, who was legally carrying a .45-caliber semiautomatic pistol, managed to get away from the other customers, including his wife, and he went to the back door to see if he could get outside and summon the police. The door, however, was locked and before Terry could take further action, one of the armed robbers spotted him and, faced with the prospect of getting shot, Terry drew his pistol and fired. Terry was grazed but the robber was hit decisively and incapacitated.

About that time, the second gunman entered the fight and traded shots with Terry, who mortally wounded him. The second gunman managed to run and stumble outside into the parking lot, where he expired. While the store manager, who had been held at gunpoint by the first robber, called police, Terry opened the walk-in refrigerator and freed the other hostages.

The two men Terry shot had criminal records. A third robber managed to escape as soon as the shooting started.

You did not read about that incident because it received very little publicity outside of the local Alabama press and one piece that appeared in the *Christian Science Monitor*. It has long been recognized by the firearms community that news which discusses the positive use of a defensive firearm by a private citizen is quite often ignored or relegated to a three-paragraph story in the back section of the local news, under a heading that might say "Police Blotter."

The press has contributed to the public perception that private citizens do not frequently use their defensive firearms successfully, when that is not true at all. Depending upon whose research one chooses – and there is a fair amount of such research available – private citizens use guns defensively upwards of two million times a year, most of the time not even firing a shot. Researchers such as Prof. Gary Kleck and John Lott have delved into this subject extensively and put the lie to arguments that armed citizens do not make a difference.

When we wrote *America Fights Back*, the authors dug through self-defense cases from all over the United States. While much of the information is anecdotal, it did establish beyond doubt that personal firearms have made a significant difference to a lot of people who may not otherwise still be alive, had they not been armed or been able to retrieve a gun to fend off a criminal attack.

In an April 2010 incident in Omaha, Nebraska, as reported by the *Omaha World-Herald*, an 18-year-old thug identified as Marquail Thomas strolled into a Walgreens. He was carrying a sawed-off shotgun in a robbery attempt with another teen, identified as Angelo Douglas, 17, who was later arrested and charged.

Thomas had a ninth grade education, and he had dropped out of school after having attended at least two high schools.

There were no police in or near the drug store when this robbery attempt unfolded, but Thomas and Douglas encountered an armed customer, Harry J. McCullough III, who had no intention of being robbed or perhaps murdered during the course of a stick-up. He fatally shot Thomas and Douglas fled. Subsequently, Thomas' mother acknowledged that her son had become someone "she hardly knew anymore," the newspaper reported.

McCullough was not charged.

In January of the same year, a Kenner, Louisiana businessman was confronted by three would-be robbers outside of his store late one Friday evening, and one of the thugs put a gun to the businessman's head. The trio of robbers pushed the man into an alley nearby, according to the *New Orleans Times-Picayune* account of the case.

The unidentified businessman, evidently fearful that he would be slain, reached into his backpack and pulled his own gun. Opening fire, he wounded one of the robbers and killed another, but the third outlaw fled. There were no policemen nearby when that incident unfolded, but instead of detectives investigating the brutal murder of a small businessman, they were able to arrest two criminals.

After their family-owned convenience store was robbed in Monroe, North Carolina, Sophea and Sophan Pich, who worked as clerks at the store, bought guns for safety. While Monroe police no doubt try to prevent and discourage criminal activity, that effort did not prevent 23-year-old Robert Young from entering Pich's Sunny Food Mart one night in late June 2010, armed with a handgun and demanding money.

According to WSOC news, the Pichs opened fire and exchanged shots with Young, who was hit several times. He later died at a nearby hospital, and in the aftermath of the investigation that cleared both clerks of any wrongdoing, Union County District Attorney John Snyder issued this statement:

"After a thorough investigation by the Monroe Police Department and a complete review of the evidence gathered, I will not press charges against the two men who bravely defended their lives against a cowardly man who wore a mask to rob the Sunny Food Mart. The honest hard working families that operate small businesses must be free from the fear of being robbed. Those that choose to rob should be filled with fear that they will suffer the same fate as the deceased. In Union County we have a no return policy on armed robbery."

An incident in South Richmond, Virginia in July 2009 illustrates the suddenness of a violent confrontation in which the legally-armed citizen hero literally walked into the middle of a crime in progress. This is far more likely to happen to an armed citizen than to a police officer simply because criminals typically try to avoid a confrontation with law enforcement.

A gunman identified as James Grooms was in the process of holding up the Golden Food Market, a convenience store in South Richmond when an unidentified friend of the store owner walked in. It was the robber's bad luck that this particular armed citizen is an open carry advocate – a person who legally carries a visible sidearm – and when he entered the store, shooting erupted.

According to an account in the *Richmond Times-Dispatch*, Grooms wounded the shopkeeper and opened fire on other store patrons but was shot by the armed Samaritan. Grooms, a convicted felon, could not legally possess the gun he was using, but that small detail has not interfered with other criminals over the years.

Grooms missed the customers he was trying to shoot, and he took a bullet in the chest. Not long after the shooting, a local council member, Reva Trammell, arrived and described the armed citizen as "a guardian angel," the newspaper noted. She said the armed man saved the lives of other store patrons.

According to the report, the good guy in this yarn was armed with a single-action revolver. After he shot Grooms, he took the bandit's gun and called police.

Remarkably, the newspaper account also revealed that police had been patrolling the street that runs in front of the convenience store, yet they were still important seconds or even minutes away when the shooting started.

The South Richmond incident was something of a publicity coup for the Open Carry movement, which made headlines early in 2010 when the Brady Campaign to Prevent Gun Violence mounted an unsuccessful campaign to force Starbucks – the Seattle-based coffee chain – to bar open carriers and ultimately all armed citizens from its coffee shops. The Brady Campaign argued that the presence of visibly armed customers frightened other coffee drinkers, especially women who might be accompanied by children, but there was no evidence that was the case. Indeed, Starbucks profits actually rose significantly during the second half of the year, essentially putting the lie to Brady Campaign claims.

Still, anecdotal incidents and financial realities do not sway some people for whom the sight of a firearm, except on the belt of a policeman, is a scary image. For whatever reason, gun prohibitionists have little or no concern about seeing an armed police officer when the appearance of an armed citizen sets off their emotional alarms.

This philosophy completely ignores the tradition of an armed citizenry on this continent even before there was a United States or a Bill of Rights. It was the armed citizens who banded together to throw off British tyranny and create this nation. Armed citizens settled and "tamed" the frontier, incrementally moving that frontier farther west, through the Ohio Valley, across the Great Plains, into Texas and the Southwest and finally to California and the Pacific Northwest and Alaska.

When outlaw gangs created havoc, it was often armed citizens that stopped them. The notorious James-Younger gang was not stopped in Northfield, Minnesota in September 1876 by a sheriff or town marshal and some deputies, but by armed private citizens who shot the gang to pieces when they tried to rob the bank. Likewise, when the Dalton gang attempted to pull the first simultaneous daylight robbery of two banks in Coffeyville, Kansas in 1892, armed citizens reinforced the town marshal, Charles Connelly, who was one of the first people killed when the shooting started. It was left to the armed townspeople to defend their community, and they killed four members of the gang and captured a badly wounded Emmett Dalton, who spent 14 years in prison before being pardoned.

United States history is filled with accounts of armed citizens defending themselves and others, even whole neighborhoods. Of course, gun prohibitionists will quickly dismiss such incidents as isolated cases from a bygone era that have nothing at all in common with what they consider "today's reality."

Perhaps someone should remind them of the day in 1966 when Texas Tower sniper Charles Whitman opened fire at the University of Texas in Austin. Several private citizens responded along with local law enforcement officers, and it was largely citizens armed with hunting rifles who kept Whitman ducking and dodging gunfire, preventing him from taking careful aim at people below. He ultimately killed 13 people, but the body count could have been much higher had not the armed citizens provided important covering fire.

Up to now, we have discussed the advantages of an armed citizenry. Rarely does anyone discuss the disadvantages of living in an environment where only police have guns. There is a proverbial "down side" to allowing only police to possess firearms; one that gun prohibitionists are loathe to address. It has to do with abuse of authority, and there may be no more blatant a recent example than an incident that occurred in early June 2011 and was captured on the dash-cam of a Canton, Ohio police officer's patrol car. When that video was released about six weeks later by gun rights advocates in Ohio, it sparked an outrage.

Shown in the video, which runs approximately 17 minutes, is an encounter between two Canton police officers and a legally-armed citizen, William Bartlett. In Ohio, an armed private citizen is required by law to immediately advise a police officer that he is carrying a firearm. In the case of this particular late-night encounter, however, Bartlett was prevented at least twice from advising Officer Daniel Harless about his concealed handgun, because Harless told him to "shut up."

The profanity-laden video was so outrageous that Canton Police Chief Dean McKimm was compelled to issue the following statement on the department's Facebook page before that page was shut down due to the volume and tone of many angry remarks:

"I want to assure our citizens that the behavior, as demonstrated in this video, is wholly unacceptable and in complete contradiction to the professional standards we demand of our officers. As such, appropriate steps were placed in motion as dictated by our standards, policies and contractual obligations. Those steps included: The officer immediately being relieved of all duty. The incident has been referred to the Internal Affairs Bureau for what will be a complete and thorough investigation. As bad as the video indicates our officer's actions were, there is a due process procedure to follow. That process is designed in the best interest of both our employees and the citizens at large. That process will be followed in this case as in all others. Anyone shown to be in violation of our rules and regulations will be help appropriately responsible as dictated by all the facts."

At one point in the video, Harless is overheard telling Bartlett that he could have executed him on the spot. In another segment, the officer tells Bartlett, "I tell you what I shoulda done. As soon as I saw your gun, I shoulda taken two steps back, pulled my Glock 40 and just put ten bullets in your ass and let you drop. And I wouldn't have lost any sleep, do you understand me?"

Throughout the confrontation, Bartlett maintained his composure and self-control, despite being arrested, threatened with a felony charge and other verbal abuse.

Harless and his partner had driven up behind Bartlett's parked car on the night of June 8. The dash-cam video shows two other people with Bartlett, a man sitting in the back seat of his car and a woman standing outside the vehicle at the curb. There were allegations that the woman was soliciting, and that the man seated in Bartlett's car was her pimp. That is not the kind of activity that warrants a response from a police officer that borders on threats of death against a citizen.

Once the video was made public, the officer was placed on administrative leave and an internal affairs investigation was launched. Bartlett retained legal counsel, and a retired Cincinnati police lieutenant, Harry Thomas, offered his services as an expert witness for the defense. Thomas, who served on the National Rifle Association Board of Directors for several years, had moved to neighboring Indiana, but he told author Workman that he was so appalled by the conduct displayed in the video that he could simply not remain silent.

That video set police public relations back decades among some gun owners, while others considered it the act of a single individual.

While the Canton incident was certainly an abuse of power, there are other black marks against the notion of only police having firearms, and there is perhaps no greater an example than the incident that unfolded in Athens, Tennessee in August 1946, documented by several sources including a grassroots gun rights organization, Jews for the Preservation of Firearms Ownership, founded by the late Aaron Zelman.

One year after the end of WWII, Tennessee had welcomed home its veterans, who had developed the notion that they were fighting to defend democracy and liberty. In Athens and Etowah in McMinn County, those ideas took a back seat to political corruption and demagoguery that had been practiced for years by politicians, including the sheriff. At election time, voters had been intimidated by sheriff's deputies, election fraud had been rampant, and pleas to the federal government, including the FBI, to intervene and investigate fell on deaf ears.

The sheriff at that time was Paul Cantrell, a powerful local political figure who ultimately won a seat in the

Tennessee State Senate, leaving his chief deputy, Pat Mansfield, to be elected in 1942 and 1944. In 1946, Cantrell once again ran for sheriff and Mansfield was the senate candidate.

However, returning war veterans had ideas of their own that included fraud-free elections and local government reform. Their candidate for sheriff was Knox Henry.

Historical accounts of the election of Aug. 1, 1946 detail how Mansfield dispatched scores of so-called "deputies," who were all armed, to various polling places to once again intimidate voters. Poll watchers were attacked and beaten by these special deputies, and one black voter named Tom Gillespie, was told indignantly by one of these deputies that he would not be permitted to vote. That conversation reportedly included a familiar racial epithet.

When Gillespie persisted, demanding that he be allowed to vote, he was beaten and then shot. He later recovered from the wound, but the fuse had been lit.

Deputies continued to interfere with the voting, and finally Mansfield seized the ballot boxes from where ballots were being counted, and took them to the jail. The veterans were having none of that, and within hours had armed themselves, with private firearms and even with some guns taken from the local National Guard and State Guard armories, including one Thompson sub-machine gun. Several veterans and supporters moved on the jail to retrieve the ballot boxes and were fired upon. Two men were hit, and it started a gun battle that lasted for nearly a half-hour. Several more people were wounded.

Early the following morning, someone threw dynamite sticks at the jail, and the subsequent explosion resulted in a surrender of the deputies inside. By sunrise, peace had returned to the community, ballots were counted honestly, Cantrell had reportedly fled into the night and the captured deputies were held in jail, apparently to prevent them from being harmed. Even the borrowed Guard firearms had been returned to their respective armories, clean. Mansfield moved to Georgia and Cantrell entered private business.

Apart from political corruption that manifests itself in an environment where police might be used as a political tool to intimidate the public, there are the more personal stories of individual abuse.

When gun control proponents argue that only police should be armed, one is compelled to ask whether they mean police like David Brame, the Tacoma, Washington police chief who – facing allegations of spousal abuse in court papers filed by his estranged wife, Crystal in 2003 – used his service pistol to fatally wound her in the parking lot before turning the gun on himself. Divorce is nothing new in the police ranks, and if one were to be candid, neither are allegations of abuse or behavior that reflects poorly on the thousands of police officers and sheriff's deputies who behave admirably and often heroically.

Simply because someone wears a badge does not give them extraordinary human traits, or make them firearms experts, or even qualify them as a good neighbor. This is not to suggest that policemen are typically ogres and worse, but blanket assertions by gun control proponents that only police should have guns demonstrate a critical lack of judgment.

A former Niagara Falls, New York police officer named Ryan G. Warme – the son of a police officer – won't be able to have a gun for the rest of his life, once he gets out of prison. Convicted in 2010 of purchasing cocaine while on duty and tipping off drug dealers about an impending raid, he also pleaded guilty to having groped a woman during a traffic stop, according to the account in the *Buffalo News*. Warme will be in federal prison for up to 13 years for his crimes, which also included making threats against a fellow inmate who was set to testify against him at trial.

In an environment where only police have guns, the worst can happen, and one need only recall the aftermath of Hurricane Katrina to understand the depths of police misbehavior. Years after that disaster, several New Orleans police officers were convicted in the shooting of unarmed citizens and the subsequent police cover-up of the crime.

The "only-cops-should-have-guns" contingent might be left speechless if asked to justify the actions of former New Orleans police officers Michael Hunter, David Warren, Greg McRae and Lt. Travis McCabe. Hunter was involved in the shooting and cover-up of the slayings of Ronald Madison and James Brissette at the Danziger Bridge in an incident that has become infamous in the Crescent City. Hunter admitted in federal court that he knowingly fired at unarmed citizens, though he steadfastly maintained that he hit nobody. His fellow officers also opened fire, and when the shooting stopped Brissette and Madison were dead and four other people had been wounded.

Warren gunned down Henry Glover in a separate incident as Glover was running away from the officer. McRae and McCabe were involved in the cover-up. Warren shot Glover from the second floor window of a building, and when Glover's brother and a friend flagged down a passing motorist to take the wounded man to an aid station, police there arrested the two men and let Glover die. Then McRae drove off with the car, with Glover's body still inside. He torched the car with the body inside and subsequently McCabe submitted a false report of the incident and lied to FBI investigators, and also committed perjury when testifying before a grand jury.

Yes, only cops like David Reeves of Riverside, California and Joseph Ferguson of Long Beach should have guns. It's easier to commit robberies and home invasions when you have guns.

Reeves pulled a 15-year prison sentence for having held up auto parts stores in Riverside and Moreno Valley, according to the *Press-Enterprise*. He used a stolen gun in at least one robbery, his last, because angry store employees overpowered him and held him for honest cops.

Ferguson and five other cops, including his brother William, were prosecuted along with several others when their home invasion robbery ring – headed by an ex-Los Angeles police officer named Ruben Palomares – was exposed. They had been robbing known drug dealers under the guise of an actual police raid. This is perhaps the ultimate abuse of authority under color of law, and for those who believe this sort of thing cannot happen in America, Ferguson and Palomares proved that it already has happened. According to newspaper accounts, they committed more than 40 burglaries and robberies over a three-year period, from 1999 to 2001.

Travel 1,500 miles north from New Orleans to Chicago and meet former Chicago Police Lt. Jon Burge. He is the disgraced officer who, according to various published accounts, routinely tortured criminal suspects and encouraged other Windy City cops to do likewise. The overwhelming majority of Burge's victims were African American men. When confronted about the allegations, he lied. But eventually, prosecutors took him down.

Burge was convicted of perjury and obstruction of justice, years after he had been fired from the department in 1993. The case outraged Chicago's black community and civil rights advocates everywhere. It was of small consolation that Burge drew a 45-year prison sentence.

A former Providence, Rhode Island cop drew a 60-year prison sentence for having picked up a drunk 19-year-old female, taking her in his police cruiser to the South Providence substation and raping her in the restroom. When the victim reported the rape, it was the same officer, Marcus Huffman, who led the investigation.

When this disgusting irony was uncovered, Huffman was successfully prosecuted. The judge in that case, Netti C. Vogel, summed up the situation: "His attack leaves the people he swore to protect feeling vulnerable and afraid." She subsequently observed, according to the account in the *Providence Journal*, that "His greatest regret was getting caught."

This is not to condemn all police officers and sheriff's deputies for the wrongdoing of some lawmen. But when gun prohibitionists make blanket assertions that "only cops should have guns," the reasoning rings hollow among firearms rights advocates who are all-too-familiar with the civil rights abuses and blatant criminal activities of some people who wear, and tarnish, the badge.

Would you advocate arming someone who kills his wife's parents and then barricades himself inside his home for several hours before finally taking his own life?

Of course, there is no way short of clairvoyance to predict whether someone who goes through life responsibly may someday snap and commit a heinous, violent act. If we cannot, through rigorous screening and training, identify whether a police officer is one day going to go over the edge, why do gun prohibitionists insist that we essentially require gun dealers to assume that responsibility when dealing with private citizens? Various gun control groups have advocated – and even tried to codify – regulations that would hold retailers, wholesalers and manufacturers responsible for the criminal acts of firearms users weeks, months or even years after a transaction. They have pursued lawsuits against gun dealers and gun makers, trying to make them financially responsible for crimes committed by people over whom they have no control.

Fortunately, the courts have wisely ruled that manufacturers are not responsible for the criminal or negligent acts of people who use their products. The same logic would apply if one wished to hold an automobile manufacturer responsible for drunken driving deaths.

Advocates of public disarmament who insist that only law enforcement officers can be trusted with firearms rarely utter a syllable when confronted with cases like that of Pierce County, Washington sheriff's deputy Allen Myron, 49. It was Myron who, in the spring of 2010, gunned down his mother-in-law and father-in-law late one Friday night, then holed up in an upstairs bedroom at his home before fatally shooting himself.

At the time, the *Tacoma News Tribune* revealed that mother-in-law Susan Multanen managed to crawl outside and call for help on her cell phone. She later died.

Myron's wife, Sara, was not at home when the shooting occurred.

It is not just murder or torture that rogue cops – the ones to whom anti-gunners would trust this nation's firearms, and the safety of their neighborhoods – engage in, but also drug trafficking, road rage and criminal assault.

The raw truth is that we hire police officers from the human race, as Jack Webb's *Dragnet* character Sgt. Joe Friday once observed. They do not instantly become heroes just by putting on a uniform, badge and gun belt. They are not automatically firearms experts because they carry one on the job. Indeed, many police officers are only moderately proficient with their firearms – good enough to pass their annual or semi-annual qualifications, but rarely do they fire those guns at any other time – and their duty sidearm may be the only gun they possess. They are not immune to drunkenness, speeding or other vices, up to and including lying under oath. Law enforcement is not a one-size-fits-all profession, so to reflexively argue that only police should have guns is a folly of ignorance.

Ask the family of Guiatree Hardat, the 22-year-old woman from Queens, New York who, in May 2007, was slain by her fiancé, Harry Rupnarine, at the time a New York City Transit Authority police officer. Rupnarine shot Miss Hardat in the back of the head with his department-issued Glock 9mm semiautomatic pistol during what the *New York Daily News* described as a "heated argument" on a public street. The quarrel, according to the newspaper account, was over money for their impending nuptials. Initially, the 39-year-old Rupnarine asserted that he had accidentally shot his fiancée while trying to protect her from a couple of armed attackers.

Keep this in perspective: Rupnarine, Tacoma Police Chief David Brame and the officers in New Orleans all had something in common: They used *department-issued* firearms to commit murder. Gun prohibitionists would have us believe that these are the "only people" who should have guns?

While the overwhelming majority of men and women in law enforcement are good citizens doing the best job they can, as with the general population, there are occasionally some very bad people in the profession, as there are in any profession.

As noted earlier in this chapter, it is rare that good cops, or even bad ones, are on hand to intervene when a violent crime erupts. There are usually only two people at the scene of a crime, the perpetrator and the victim(s). Police may show up quickly, not so quickly or, depending upon the department, not at all, and certainly not in time to actually prevent the crime from being committed.

For those who are delusional enough to believe that they will be invariably rescued from harm "in the nick of time" by the police, there are emergency rooms and trauma centers, medical examiners and coroners, and lots of white chalk for outlines. For everyone else, there exists the fundamental right to keep and bear arms.

Sometimes, the "only cops should have guns" advocates dismiss self-defense arguments by countering that would-be crime victims merely need to run away. That's a tidy theory, but it does not translate well to real life. Indeed, this philosophy can be entirely discredited by the story of a western Pennsylvania double-amputee who fatally shot a home invader early on the morning of Jan. 2, 2011 because he not only had nowhere to run, he had no legs so running was out of the question.

The *Pittsburgh Tribune-Review* identified the wheelchair-bound would-be victim as Rocco Bombara, who was at home with his sons and some friends watching television. Bombara always carries a handgun because, as a neighbor observed to the newspaper, "Around here, if you're disabled, you're a target."

A 19-year-old thug identified as Lairy Evans James-Watson tried crawling through one of Bombara's apartment windows. When the double-amputee confronted James-Watson, who was about halfway through the window – the teen gunman opened fire with a rifle. One of his bullets struck his intended victim in the hand, but apparently not his gun hand.

Affirming that James-Watson had made a fatal error in the victim selection process, Bombara returned fire, killing the gunman, whom he apparently had never before set eyes on, the newspaper indicated.

Responding police were minutes away, but the incident was over in seconds, with the would-be victim successfully defending himself and his teenage children and guests. What would have happened to them if only the police, and the criminal, had guns?

They would have become statistics that gun control advocates would use to call for more restrictive gun laws, under the pretense that one more statutory limitation on the rights of law-abiding gun owners would somehow prevent people like Lairy Evans James-Watson from arming themselves for the purpose of committing crimes.

It is important to keep this in perspective, however: None of these incidents has any relevance to gun prohibitionists. Such incidents are dismissed out of hand or ignored altogether. Public disarmament advocates have no intention of seeking to justify or defend their agenda. They merely want their agenda imposed, and facts contrary to what they advocate simply do not matter.

Four

GUNS DO NOT BELONG ON CAMPUS

Q. *Aren't high school and college campuses made safer for learning by declaring them to be 'gun-free zones'?*

Virginia Tech, Northern Illinois University, Appalachian Law School, University of Washington, Columbine High School, Pearl High School, Thurston High School, Foss High School, Red Lake High School, Heath High School; all of these places have two things in common.

They are the scenes of school shootings. They are also "gun-free school zones," essentially making them target-rich, low-risk environments otherwise known as "victim disarmament zones" for kill-crazy monsters, some of whom shared one saving grace: They killed themselves, sparing the police or the courts from doing it, and sparing the taxpayers the enormous costs of trying these people, finding them guilty and sentencing them to life in prison or death, the latter which often translates to many years of legal maneuvers, appeals and more appeals. Others, such as Oregon's Kip Kinkel who murdered his parents – both educators – before going to Thurston High School in Springfield and opening fire, were taken into custody and imprisoned without possibility of parole. In Kinkel's case, that happened only after he had been soundly beaten and restrained by some classmates, one of whom he had shot in the chest just seconds before.

In our earlier collaboration, *America Fights Back: Armed Self-Defense in a Violent Age*, the authors detailed the Thurston High School shooting, along with the events at Virginia Tech and Appalachian Law School. These incidents are well-documented and there is no need to gratuitously repeat the details here, though we will talk briefly about the Appalachian Law School incident later in this chapter.

A comprehensive 2010 report prepared by the Department of Education (DOE), U.S. Secret Service and Federal Bureau of Investigation titled *Campus Attacks: Targeted Violence Affecting Institutions of Higher Education* suggests that because college campuses are spread out and encompass multiple buildings, campus shootings may not be as preventable as claimed by advocates of gun free zones. This report looked at violent incidents that occurred at institutions of higher learning (IHEs) between January 1, 1900 and December 31, 2008, a total of 108 years of data.

The report revealed that in all that time, there had been a total of 272 incidents that resulted in 281 fatalities and 247 reported injuries, including such notorious cases as Virginia Tech and Charles Whitman's rampage at the University of Texas at Austin.

According to Students for Concealed Carry on Campus (SCCC), founded within 24 hours of the Virginia Tech massacre, in 2008 alone there were 60 murders, 3,287 rapes, 5,026 physical assaults and 4,562 robberies on college campuses around the country. Yet with that available data, college and university administrations are adamantly opposed to allowing students to legally carry firearms on campus, even if they have concealed carry permits or licenses, and even if they can demonstrate they have received training in firearm safety and the use of force.

Contrary to the rhetoric one might hear from those opposed to concealed carry anywhere, and particularly on college campuses, SCCC does not, nor has it ever, advocated arming students. Their focus has always been simply allowing those students and instructors already licensed to carry to have their defensive firearms with them on campus, as they would carry them anywhere else. Opponents have tried to color this debate with fairly transparent predictions that drunken fraternity parties would erupt with gunfire, and that teenage freshmen would pose a danger to other students, when in truth those students could not get a concealed carry permit because they are under age.

Only in cases where campus administrators have had to be essentially dragged "kicking and screaming" have they permitted guns on campus, or done so under court order. College campuses in Utah and Colorado were compelled by the courts to allow students and staff to have concealed firearms. It came as no surprise to SCCC and gun rights organizations that these changes in regulations were not followed by outbreaks of violence, despite predictions to the contrary by spokespersons for the gun prohibition lobby. However, academic resistance to allowing legally-licensed students or administrators to be armed on college campuses has remained fierce, and most states continue prohibitions against firearms on campus.

Part of the Secret Service/FBI report included data from the DOE covering crimes reported by private and public institutions to the agency from 2005 through 2008, and it is revealing. In all, there were 235,599 crimes reported including 174 murders and non-negligent manslaughters of which 80 occurred on campus and 82 happened on adjacent public property. Of the on-campus slayings, 13 occurred in residence halls. Only a dozen happened at non-campus facilities. In addition, 9.2 percent of the crimes were aggravated assaults, 8.4 percent were robberies and 5.9 percent were rape.

SCCC maintains that females are "disproportionately at risk" under the current circumstances, "because a majority of college patrons (57 percent of students and 54 percent of faculty) are female."

SCCC mounted efforts to change campus policy that would allow legally-licensed college students or faculty to carry firearms on campus. Administrators – perhaps concerned that they might appear to be acknowledging that their campuses are not safe, and thus lose important benefactor contributions, or maybe because they are politically and philosophically far to the left of center compared to the general public – consistently dismissed such requests. Instead of allowing legally armed students, universities contended that they have armed police or unarmed security officers on patrol.

The University of Washington, for example, has its own police department and they carry guns, and have been armed for many years. Their presence did not protect 26-year-old Rebecca Jane Griego, a program coordinator for the UW's Department of Urban Design and Planning. Her ex-boyfriend, an illegal alien named Jonathan Rowan, 41, against whom she had taken out a protection order, was able to come onto the campus and murder Griego in her office on April 2, 2007 with a stolen handgun. Rowan shot Griego at almost point blank range before turning the gun on himself. Rowan had been stalking Griego, and there was a history of domestic abuse when they were living together earlier in the year.

It was not the first time that armed police did *not* prevent a killing at the UW campus. News archives of the *Seattle Times* recall earlier incidents that included the June 28, 2000 slaying of a university pathologist by a student who was about to flunk out of the university's pathology program.

Eleven years earlier, in July 1989, Marjan Mohseninia and Abraham Sharif-Kashani were gunned down in a university parking lot by Mohseninia's ex-boyfriend, Azizolla Mazooni, of California. The newspaper recalled that he had actually retained a private investigator to find Mohseninia. Mazooni was later convicted of two counts of second-degree murder.

A third incident in December 1979 involved the slaying of Larry Duerkson by his lover and roommate,

Roger Cutsinger, on the campus. This was an apparent murder for insurance. Cutsinger was the beneficiary on a $500,000 insurance policy Duerkson had taken out.

Virginia Tech has its own police department, with this mission statement: *The Virginia Tech Police Department strives to enhance the safety and quality of life for students, faculty, staff and visitors through effective law enforcement and proactive crime prevention in partnership with the university community.*

One might argue that the department failed in that mission miserably on April 16, 2007 when Sueng Hui-Cho killed two people in West Ambler Johnston Hall. About two hours later – while the police were questioning another student who had nothing to do with the killings, but was a friend of one of the victims and apparently was a known gun owner and shooter – he entered Norris Hall and killed 30 more people before taking his own life. The authors discussed this horrible case in detail in our earlier collaboration, *America Fights Back: Armed Self-defense in a Violent Age*.

By logging onto the department's web site, visitors can see various crime reports, as can anybody looking for similar information from other college and university police agencies around the country.

Making it easier for a would-be killer to carry out his fantasy by disarming his potential victims seems an egregiously stupid policy, and some might even consider it criminally negligent. However, as will be demonstrated in a moment, the Virginia Supreme Court sees it differently. As SCCC has determined by breaking down the data contained in the *Campus Attacks* report, of the 79 percent of attacks that occurred on campuses, 28 percent of those happened in dorms, 27 percent in parking lots or on the grounds, and 26 percent in campus buildings.

What does that tell you? This statistical breakdown demonstrates that a criminal act can occur anywhere on campus. So, the question must be asked, why do college administrators adopt policies that make it easy for such crimes to occur?

The situation is somewhat different on K-12 public school campuses, where there is typically only one building with perhaps a separate gym, or buildings with several classroom wings branching away from a main corridor. Adoption of "zero tolerance" regulations across the country has not stopped young killers, and in the process, the policy has been occasionally extremely abusive. Documented cases of elementary school youngsters being suspended because they had a tiny toy gun from an action figure have occasionally reminded the public that zero tolerance has translated to zero common sense, and in a way, absolute authority. We all know what absolute power can do: It can corrupt absolutely, even at the level of elementary school teacher or administrator.

These policies have entangled students living in rural school districts, where hunting remains a strong component of the lifestyle. Among previous generations, it was not unusual in rural America to find high school students leave campus at the end of the day and go hunting, having locked a rifle or shotgun in the trunk of a car or behind the seat of a pickup truck. Indeed, many schools had rifle teams, and it was not out of the ordinary to see members of the team gearing up one afternoon a week or twice a month after school with their shooting jackets and pads, and cased rifles, a vision that might horrify zero tolerance advocates.

Today, students who inadvertently leave a firearm or hunting knife or ammunition in their vehicles face suspension or expulsion. In some cases, they may even wind up with a criminal record that could preclude them from entering college or the military, or qualifying for certain jobs, and perhaps preventing them from ever again owning a firearm legally, depending upon how gun laws may change in the future.

This does not have to happen, and really should not be happening, and in some cases where school administrators and local school boards use their heads and allow common sense to prevail, the results can be gratifying. A celebrated case in western Montana late in 2010 provided some reassurance that rural common sense trumps urban nonsense every time. In that case, a 16-year-old high school honor student inadvertently left an unloaded hunting rifle locked in the trunk of her car following a Thanksgiving hunting trek with her family.

A few days later, upon learning that school authorities were searching the parking lot with a specially-trained dog that sniffs out drugs and firearms, the teenager – who was also a member of the junior varsity cheerleading staff – quickly advised school authorities about the rifle. Because the school was in lockdown during the search, she could not make the short trip home to put the gun where it belonged. She was suspended, and that ignited a firestorm of anger throughout the Pacific Northwest.

However, cooler heads prevailed because in western Montana it is not unusual for people to leave a hunting rifle in their vehicle. In some communities, it would be more unusual to not have a gun in the car. Several days after the suspension, the school board met in a jam-packed hearing, held in a school gymnasium because of the overflow crowd of local citizens (the kind who vote on school bond issues and levies). The suspension was lifted, the young lady apologized for her mistake and school administrators promised to help her catch up on her school work. The entire incident was resolved before Christmas. In Montana they do things differently; a lesson that should rub off on school administrations elsewhere.

In the aftermath of the Columbine mass shooting in April, 1999, police agencies have adopted a new philosophy about responding to such a situation. There was considerable public anger that Colorado police did not move in fast enough, but waited outside the high school while enough officers arrived to provide what might be defined as a massive dynamic entry.

Columbine changed response policy to make it more of a priority to get inside and confront an active shooter, thus perhaps taking him out or at least keeping him pinned down until reinforcements arrive, while at the same time preventing the loss of further human life. This strategy certainly played out at a non-school shooting at Salt Lake City's Trolley Square in February 2007. A gunman opened fire there killing five people and wounding four others before an off-duty police officer from a nearby community engaged the shooter in a gun battle and prevented him from gunning down other victims until on-duty officers arrived and killed him.

This should have provided a lesson for public shopping mall managers. Many such facilities ban the carrying of firearms even by licensed private citizens because they are private property despite being public venues. Some state concealed carry statutes allow for such bans; a compromise written into the legislation to mollify some lawmakers who may have reservations about approving a more sensible law that would exempt legally-licensed citizens from such prohibitions.

But mall managers are resistant, and in the wake of a Virginia State Supreme Court ruling in January 2011, so are college and university administrators. In a case called *DiGiacinto v. Rector*, the Virginia high court ruled that although the state constitution included a right to keep and bear arms provision that protects an individual right, public universities are recognized as "sensitive places" where guns might be prohibited, as explained in the U.S. Supreme Court's ruling in *District of Columbia v. Dick Anthony Heller* in 2008. That was the ruling that defined the Second Amendment as protective of an individual civil right.

Gun rights researcher Eugene Volokh, who manages an Internet forum called The Volokh Conspiracy, wrote in his book *Implementing the Right to Keep and Bear Arms in Self-Defense*, "It's not clear to me how other public property should be treated: Should the government be allowed to ban guns on government-owned recreational land, whether a city park or a national park, either by insisting that people who want to use the land must waive their right to bear arms, or by otherwise concluding that there is no right to bear arms in such places? As a condition of going onto a public university campus, which might have a considerable amount of open space and parking areas where crime is not uncommon? In public university dorm rooms, where one state attorney general's opinion suggests gun possession is constitutionally protected? As a condition of going onto a public primary or secondary school campus, or into a government office building, especially when this requires walking unarmed through a potentially dangerous parking structure? Courts need to work out a government-as-proprietor doctrine for the right to bear arms much as they have done for the freedom of speech."

The Virginia opinion, written by Justice S. Bernard Goodwyn, referred to the *Heller* ruling, and the subsequent Supreme Court ruling, *McDonald v. City of Chicago*, which both prominently note that the Second Amendment is not an "absolute right" but can be subject to some regulation.

Complicating the issue was the fact that the plaintiff in the Virginia case, Rudolph DiGiacinto, was not a student or employee of George Mason University, the subject of the lawsuit. He merely visits the campus to utilize its various resources, including the library. He wanted to not only carry a firearm into the buildings he was visiting, but to on-campus events and he argued that the university lacked statutory authority to regulate firearms on its campus.

The court said otherwise.

However, as history has proven too many times, simply because courts say colleges and universities, and public schools for that matter, can prohibit firearms does not automatically mean they are safe or that it is good public policy. The "gun free school zone" debate continues to rage, with both sides claiming the higher ground in the argument. Columbine and other school shootings have demonstrated that the argument may be heated and filled with rhetoric, but it is entirely academic. In the event of a shooting by a determined individual, all of those verbal and written arguments and rules do not stop bullets.

In January 2011, a 17-year-old Omaha, Nebraska high school student named Robert Butler Jr. was escorted off the campus at Millard South High School, after having been cited for driving a car on the school's track and football field on New Year's Day. According to the Associated Press, Butler – the son of an Omaha police detective – returned to the school a few hours later and shot Principal Curtis Case and Assistant Principal Vicki Kaspar. Kaspar later died of her wounds. The school had an unarmed security guard, but he took cover and was not shot as Butler walked away, even though the teen aimed the gun at him. Butler also shot at a school custodian, but missed.

Firearms rights opponents have perpetuated the argument that schools are safer without firearms, and yet when these gun free zones are violated and lives are lost, they assume no responsibility for their lobbying efforts which created the "gun free zone" myth, but instead blame the "gun lobby" and "lax gun laws." The same is true after virtually any high-profile shooting, including the shooting of Arizona Congresswoman Gabrielle "Gabby" Giffords at a shopping mall in Tucson in January 2011. While Giffords survived the horrible shooting, six others including a federal judge and 9-year-old girl, did not.

In response, one congressman, Rep. Peter King (R-NY) suggested creating a 1,000-foot "gun free zone" around any member of Congress. Such a prohibition would be impossible to enforce, and quite possibly interfere with campaigning by some members, who like to show off their support of the Second Amendment by holding shooting events that double as campaign fund raisers.

In the private sector, the gun prohibition lobby almost immediately pulled out its political agenda, literally before police had processed the Giffords shooting crime scene. Instead of placing blame on the shooter, gun prohibitionists quickly defined the argument as one involving high-capacity ammunition magazines.

When making arguments against allowing firearms on campus, the arguments are different but the goal is the same: Keep people disarmed. This approach carries with it what might be best called "collateral damage" because crime often occurs in neighborhoods adjacent to a university campus where perpetrators have a reasonable expectation that their intended victim is not armed.

To illustrate this, look at the aforementioned University of Washington in Seattle and the adjacent University District, through which University Avenue runs north-to-south. It is a hub of activity day and night throughout the school year and even during the summer when the university population falls because of the seasonal drop in enrollment.

In October 2010, a series of brazen robberies began occurring in the University District, usually in the evening and late into the night, but there was one that occurred in broad daylight. Single females walking alone were targeted by male and female thugs who would drive up to someone, jump out and grab a purse or demand money. Sometimes a gun was displayed, sometimes not. Many, if not most of the victims were co-eds at the university, and they could not legally carry defensive firearms even if they wanted to, if they were coming back from class or studying late. The holdups continued through the winter.

This is not unlike the environment around many urban college campuses. Population demographics of such neighborhoods tend to be younger and politically liberal, so many times firearms possession is simply out of the question. Thieves know the odds are in their favor, and an armed robber can operate with confidence that he will very likely have the only gun at the scene of his crime.

Despite much evidence that gun-free environments act like magnets for criminal activity, advocates of public disarmament – for whatever reason – cling to their belief that the absence of legally-carried personal protection firearms is a good thing. To acknowledge otherwise would be to publicly admit that they have been wrong, and no academic institution is going to make such an admission. Instead, they offer platitudes about maintaining a safe environment for students, staff and faculty, and insist that whatever criminal situation might erupt, they are prepared and equipped to handle it.

Earlier in this chapter, we discussed SCCC's report about crime on campus, taken from the FBI's *Campus Attacks: Targeted Violence Affecting Institutions of Higher Education.* The group noted that 21 percent of the attacks or slayings in that report were random. That's nearly a fourth of all the campus attacks reported, and it means that if attcked one stands a good chance of being attacked or killed on campus by a total stranger.

We also noted earlier that women are more likely to be at risk of attack than men, simply because they outnumber males on a typical campus. In most cases, they present the weaker target to an attacker, and thus the odds rise even more that they will be the victims. So, instead of asking whether campuses are safer by banning firearms possession by those legally able to carry guns anywhere else, one should be asking why college and university administrators adamantly resist efforts to give these would-be victims an opportunity to have the tools to defend themselves in case of an attack.

This issue is hardly new. Recall the mid-1970s and the murder spree of Theodore Robert Bundy. His primary victims were college coeds. Among the dead were University of Washington students Lynda Ann Healy and Georgeann Hawkins, Evergreen State College student Donna Gail Manson, Central Washington University coed Susan Rancourt, and Oregon State University student Kathy Parks. After he left Washington and went to Utah, he killed Susan Curtis, a student at Brigham Young University who disappeared from the campus. Among his last victims were Florida State University students Lisa Levy and Margaret Bowman, killed as they slept in their rooms at the Chi Omega sorority.

Bundy was a prolific murderer and, like Gary Ridgway, the infamous "Green River Killer" who murdered at least 49 women, he didn't use a gun, proving that not all campus killers are gunmen. One is tempted to wonder what "might have been" had one of Bundy's victims been armed.

What happens in the rare event – due to restrictive campus codes – when armed students are able to intervene? As noted at the beginning of this chapter, the authors discussed such a case in *America Fights Back: Armed Self-Defense in a Violent Age*. The January 2002 shooting at the Appalachian School of Law in Virginia provides perhaps the best rebuttal to those who insist that armed intervention by private citizens would not be the proper solution to a campus shooting.

A 42-year-old former student from Nigeria, Peter Odighizuwa, called "Peter O" by others because of the difficulty in pronouncing his name, had flunked out once and was about to be dropped again when he showed up carrying a .380-caliber pistol. After telling Professor Dale Rubin to pray for him, Odighizuwa went to the offices of Dean Anthony Sutin and Prof. Thomas Blackwell, and shot them both fatally at close range. He then turned the gun on a student, Angela Dales, shooting her dead, and fired shots that wounded three other students.

Two students, who happened to be off-duty police officers from out-of-state jurisdictions – essentially making them armed private citizens like anyone else – independently raced to their cars and retrieved handguns. Students Tracy Bridges and Mikael Gross then – again independent from one another – approached Odighizuwa from different directions. Bridges yelled at the gunman and ordered him to drop his pistol, which he immediately did before being physically taken down by a third student, Ted Besen, and several others.

Besen, however, has said Odighizuwa dropped his gun before Bridges and Gross closed in on him. Some witnesses contend that his pistol was empty, but neither armed student had any way of knowing that.

Firearms researcher John Lott subsequently analyzed reportage after the incident, and discovered that the press accounts almost uniformly ignored or omitted, the fact that two armed students intervened to halt the shooting.

According to SCCC, 26 colleges allowed concealed carry on their campuses at the time of this writing. That number included all public universities in Utah, and several campuses in Colorado including all of their branches. The total comes to more than 70 different college campuses.

Here is one thing that is rarely discussed by gun prohibitionists and opponents of firearms on campus. "According to crime statistics and inquiries to campus officials," SCCC says on their website, "there hasn't been a single reported instance of shootouts, accidents or heated confrontations resulting from concealed carry on campus."

Indeed, the crime rate at Colorado State University actually declined after carry was allowed on that campus.

"While no one can irrefutably claim this is due to concealed carry," SCCC acknowledged, "we can at least state with certainty that *allowing concealed carry does not increase risks to a campus population* and may even help."

What gun opponents appear to invariably overlook in this debate is the fact that these firearms would be concealed. That is, nobody would see them. The adage "out of sight, out of mind" would seem to apply, though one certainly could predict that campus gun prohibitionists would still disdain the practice, even if they had no idea whether any of their students or colleagues was armed.

The purpose of concealed carry on campus is purely defensive. Students and faculty who advocate carrying firearms on campus have no intention of intimidating or frightening anyone. Their single concern is about *not* being a victim.

Five

LAX GUN LAWS FUEL MEXICAN DRUG WAR

Q. *Shouldn't we tighten our gun laws and renew the ban on 'assault weapons' to stop the flow of guns to violent drug cartels in Mexico?*

Beginning in early 2009, the Obama administration and its supporters in the gun prohibition lobby launched a campaign to revive the ban on semiautomatic modern sporting rifles, and institute new regulations on gun shows by casting blame on American gun laws for allowing guns from this country to fuel the violent drug wars in northern Mexico.

From the outset, the administration and the press began reporting and repeating – obviously without checking the facts – that up to 90 percent of the guns recovered by Mexican authorities at crime scenes came from the United States. Once the lie was repeated enough times, it became the truth, much like the principle expressed by a small town newspaper editor imparted to James Stewart in the film *The Man Who Shot Liberty Valance.*

"This is the West," the editor observed. "When legend becomes fact, print the legend."

There has been enough evidence, however, even from the federal Bureau of Alcohol, Tobacco, Firearms and Explosives (ATF), that the assertion that 90 percent of Mexican crime guns come from the United States simply proves false. At best, a fraction of the firearms used in Mexico by warring cartels have been traced to this country. The claim appears to be a fabrication, based loosely on information that had been selectively exaggerated and, quite possibly, deliberately misinterpreted.

But proving this and acknowledging that the assertion is in error is not the point and never have been. As former White House chief of staff Rahm Emanuel was fond of observing, "Never let an emergency go to waste." And this is precisely what gun prohibitionists have endeavored to accomplish, largely by ignoring the facts.

In April 2009, when the Obama administration's "campaign by trial balloon" to renew the ban on so-called "assault weapons" was in its early stages, Fox News reporters William Lajeunesse and Maxim Lott aired a report that amounted to a face slap at Attorney General Eric Holder, Secretary of State Hillary Rodham Clinton and others who had been mouthing the administration line about the number of guns recovered in Mexico.

Said Lajeunesse as his lead:

> *EXCLUSIVE: You've heard this shocking "fact" before -- on TV and radio, in newspapers, on the Internet and from the highest politicians in the land: 90 percent of the weapons used to commit crimes in Mexico come from the United States.*
>
> *– Secretary of State Hillary Clinton said it to reporters on a flight to Mexico City.*
>
> *– CBS newsman Bob Schieffer referred to it while interviewing President Obama.*
>
> *– California Sen. Dianne Feinstein said at a Senate hearing: "It is unacceptable to have 90 percent of the guns that are picked up in Mexico and used to shoot judges, police officers and mayors ... come from the United States."*

– *William Hoover, assistant director for field operations at the Bureau of Alcohol, Tobacco, Firearms and Explosives, testified in the House of Representatives that "there is more than enough evidence to indicate that over 90 percent of the firearms that have either been recovered in, or interdicted in transport to Mexico, originated from various sources within the United States."*

There's just one problem with the 90 percent "statistic" and it's a big one:

It's just not true.

In fact, it's not even close. The fact is, only 17 percent of guns found at Mexican crime scenes have been traced to the U.S.

In this report, an ATF spokeswoman even tried to set the record straight.

Gun rights advocates have repeatedly argued that prohibitionists have essentially played with data in an effort to revive and pursue their long standing agenda, which is to renew the ban on so-called "assault weapons" and pass "gun show background check" legislation that would hold gun show promoters criminally liable for any technical violations, even if they had no knowledge or control over the violators. This is one tactic, say gun show operators, the government would employ to put gun shows out of business, thus eliminating one of the country's traditional gathering places for firearms collectors, gun rights activists and other firearms enthusiasts.

Thus, the effort does not simply involve stopping criminals from buying firearms – a demonstrably false impression invented by gun prohibitionists to portray gun shows as "arms bazaars" for criminals and terrorists – but to curtail the opportunity for gun owners to congregate and discuss politics and related subjects. In a way, this is a First Amendment issue, though one would be hard pressed to ever get a gun control proponent to admit that.

Likewise, no gun prohibitionist is going to acknowledge that they are determined to find any excuse to curtail gun shows, even if it means deliberately exaggerating facts or making them up from whole cloth. The April 2009 Lajeunesse report that attempted to widely reveal the truth was a rare departure from the myth. It would be almost two years before another journalist would provide a detailed rebuttal to the 90-percent myth.

Writing for *Stratfor Global Intelligence* on-line in early 2011, author Scott Stewart essentially destroyed the argument that American firearms laws and U.S.-based firearms retailers were responsible for the majority of guns involved in the Mexican drug wars. According to Stewart, "...the 90 percent number was derived from a June 2009 U.S. Government Accountability Office (GAO) report to Congress on U.S. efforts to combat arms trafficking to Mexico."

"According to the GAO report," Stewart detailed, "some 30,000 firearms were seized from criminals by Mexican authorities in 2008. Of these 30,000 firearms, information pertaining to 7,200 of them (24 percent) was submitted to the U.S. Bureau of Alcohol, Tobacco, Firearms and Explosives (ATF) for tracing. Of these 7,200 guns, only about 4,000 could be traced by the ATF, and of these 4,000, some 3,480 (87 percent) were shown to have come from the United States.

"This means," he continued, "that the 87 percent figure relates to the number of weapons submitted by the Mexican government to the ATF that could be successfully traced and not from the total number of weapons seized by Mexican authorities or even from the total number of weapons submitted to the ATF for tracing. In fact, the 3,480 guns positively traced to the United States equals less than 12 percent of the total arms seized in Mexico in 2008 and less than 48 percent of all those submitted by the Mexican government to the ATF for tracing. This means that almost 90 percent of the guns seized in Mexico in 2008 were not traced back to the United States.

"The remaining 22,800 firearms seized by Mexican authorities in 2008," Stewart explained, "were not traced for a variety of reasons. In addition to factors such as bureaucratic barriers and negligence, many of the weapons seized by Mexican authorities either do not bear serial numbers or have had their serial numbers altered or obliterated. It is also important to understand that the Mexican authorities simply don't bother to submit some classes of weapons to the ATF for tracing. Such weapons include firearms they identify as coming from their own military or police forces, or guns that they can trace back themselves as being sold through the Mexican Defense Department's Arms and Ammunition Marketing Division (UCAM). Likewise, they do not ask ATF to trace military ordnance from third countries like the South Korean fragmentation grenades commonly used in cartel attacks.

"Of course, some or even many of the 22,800 firearms the Mexicans did not submit to ATF for tracing may have originated in the United States," he acknowledged. "But according to the figures presented by the GAO, there is no evidence to support the assertion that 90 percent of the guns used by the Mexican cartels come from the United States — especially when not even 50 percent of those that were submitted for tracing were ultimately found to be of U.S. origin."

That was not the kind of information that American gun prohibitionists wished to see widely circulated. There is speculation that, had Stewart's report supported the 90 percent claim, it would have been leading news on all three evening network news broadcasts.

And then there was "Project Gunrunner," the controversial ATF operation that allowed the creation of a debacle in Arizona known as "Operation Fast and Furious" under which the agency allowed multiple transactions involving more than two dozen suspected gun runners and straw purchasers to buy hundreds of firearms from several federally-licensed firearms retailers – with their cooperation. A majority of those guns may have been put into circulation south of the border. We will discuss Operation Fast and Furious more in Chapter Eleven.

"Gunrunner" began as a pilot project in 2005 in Laredo, Texas. A little over two years later, in January

2008, ATF decided to expand the operation, adding agents and inspectors, and spreading out through the southern border states, according to a history of the operation found on Wikipedia. The project really gained momentum in the fall of 2009 and through much of 2010 following media reports and assertions from the Obama administration that a "flood" of U.S. firearms was flowing south. But in the process of ostensibly stemming that flow of guns, it appears the project got out of control and actually allowed thousands of firearms to illicitly reach Mexico or get into the hands of drug gangs on this side of the border.

Tragically this operation was linked to the December 2010 murder of Border Patrol Agent Brian Terry ten miles north of Nogales, Arizona. Investigators recovered two guns at the scene of the shootout that had been purchased 11 months before by one of the chief suspects in the Gunrunner sting; one of many purchases that ATF officials allowed to "walk" on the presumption that agents working the case could track where the guns went. Ironically, or perhaps not, the suspect was arrested by federal authorities on the day following the gunfight. What happened in the wake of the Terry slaying, however, became regarded by many in the firearms community as an attempted cover-up, and their opinion was evidently shared by a United States senator. Ultimately, it became an embarrassing chapter for a federal agency that was already held in rather low esteem by the firearms community.

The fallout from Project Gunrunner, and in particular its offshoot "Operation Fast and Furious" was what CBS reporter Sharyl Attkisson described as "a scandal so large, some insiders say it surpasses the shoot-out at Ruby Ridge and the deadly siege at Waco." While CBS quoted a former ATF agent who estimated that as many as 2,500 firearms were allowed to "walk" across the border to Mexico because ATF officials in Phoenix, Arizona – where "Fast and Furious" was based – refused to allow field agents to intercept the suspected gunrunners, other estimates about guns going south have been higher. One ATF insider likened the estimate to a high-profile drug bust that pulls in a thousand pounds of cocaine, while "a hundred thousand pounds got through somewhere else."

As revelations about the Gunrunner scandal emerged, it was became obvious that the problem was not confined to Arizona.

There was also trouble with guns being allowed into the black market in Texas. This situation involved one of the state's biggest and most famous firearms retailers, Carter's Country in Houston. Making matters worse for the ATF, the store's attorney was Dick Deguerin, a respected Texas lawyer with a reputation for being straightforward. He told Houston's Fox News affiliate about the involvement of his clients in this gun smuggling operation.

"They were told to go through with sales of three or more assault rifles at the same time," Deguerin recalled in a statement to the reporter. "They went through with the sales because the ATF told them to go through with the sales."

The attorney was careful to note that Carter's Country invariably notified ATF about suspicious sales. It set off alarms when the agency said to allow the transactions.

According to the Fox News report, this type of transaction is called a "controlled delivery," and is utilized in drug trafficking investigations. ATF would not admit using this investigative technique and instead essentially said nothing. When the affiliate sought a comment from ATF, a spokeswoman in Washington, D.C. referred questions to two spokesmen, who did not return calls or reply to e-mails.

Author Workman experienced the same silence, from one of the same designated spokesmen, during his examination of the "Project Gunrunner" controversy. Early in the course of covering the story for *Gun Week* and for his on-line column at Examiner.com, he was told that only one individual was speaking for ATF on that matter. He quickly learned that the spokesman wasn't really speaking at all.

It would soon become evident that this silence was not exclusively directed at members of the working press.

Early in 2011, Iowa Senator Charles Grassley, ranking Republican on the Senate Judiciary Committee, became curious about reports from confidential sources that hundreds of firearms involved in the "Project Gunrunner" investigation had been taken across the border. Grassley's staff was able to speak to ATF agents to confirm their concerns that this operation had gone seriously wrong.

In a letter to then-Acting ATF Director Kenneth Melson, Sen. Grassley said there were serious allegations that ATF's Gunrunner sting operation "may have become careless, if not negligent, in implementing...strategy." He asked for an ATF briefing on the case.

Instead, Grassley received a letter from Assistant Attorney General Ronald Weich that made him bristle. In that letter, Weich denied that the agency had allowed guns to get into the wrong hands in what became known during the Watergate era as a "non-denial denial."

"ATF makes ever effort to interdict weapons that have been purchased illegally and prevent their transportation to Mexico," Weich wrote.

But Weich went one step farther, and it may have been a step too far, when he denied assertions that ATF officials in Arizona had tried to retaliate against the field agents who cooperated with Grassley's inquiry. And then he wrote something that infuriated Grassley and smacked of a cover-up.

"We also want to protect investigations and the law enforcement personnel who directly conduct them from inappropriate political influence," Weich stated. "For this reason, we respectfully request that Committee staff not contact law enforcement personnel seeking information about pending criminal investigations, including the investigation into the death of...Agent Brian Terry."

That response infuriated Grassley and only made him more determined to find the truth.

Months later, when Weich appeared before Congress to offer testimony on Operation Fast and Furious, he was challenged on the truthfulness of that statement. He would only say that the situation was under investigation.

Truth is sometimes an elusive prize, especially when dealing with an emotional subject like gun control. The fact remains that gun prohibitionists were simply wrong, and perhaps deliberately misleading, with their repeated claim that 90 percent of the guns recovered from Mexican crime scenes originally came from the United States. Even ATF officials disavowed the claim, though their explanations that put the data in perspective were almost uniformly ignored by the mainstream press.

Compare the government's conduct in the "Fast-and-Furious" controversy to what happened in the investigation of the slaying of Immigration and Customs (ICE) agent Jaime Zapata in northern Mexico in mid-February 2011, about the same time that the Gunrunner stories were breaking. Zapata was murdered, and his partner seriously wounded, while driving on a highway – unarmed under Mexican law that prohibits foreign law enforcement from carrying sidearms – when they were ambushed by suspected members of a drug cartel.

One of the guns recovered at the scene was traced back to a gun shop in Joshua, Texas, a town about 20 miles south of Fort Worth. Arrested in that case were three men, including the person who had purchased the firearm from a licensed dealer at a gun show in Fort Worth in October 2010. The same three men, brothers Otilio and Ranferi Osorio and their next door neighbor, Kelvin Leon Morrison, were stopped by the authorities in November 2010 apparently trying to smuggle 40 guns across the border at Laredo.

All of those guns had been apparently purchased at retail outlets, as in the Gunrunner investigation, and the serial numbers had been defaced, which is a federal crime. However, thanks to modern science, those serial numbers could be recovered, and at least three of the firearms were traced to Morrison. He was also linked to another gun that was recovered by authorities in LaPryor, Texas in August 2010. The guns were confiscated and never reached Mexico, but by that time, the gun found at the Zapata crime scene may have already crossed the border.

This incident put the Osorio brothers and Morrison on federal radar, however. After Zapata was murdered, Mexican authorities asked ATF to trace the firearms and they scored. The gun in question had been purchased by Otilio Osorio from Off Duty Armory. Owner Jim Terrill told author Workman that Osorio bought the gun individually; that is, it was a single purchase and not part of a batch of guns, as the alleged conspirators in the Gunrunner case had repeatedly purchased in Arizona.

The transaction occurred before Osorio's interception in Laredo a month later. According to Terrill, the background check on Osorio cleared his purchase.

It is not known how many other guns linked to the Osorio brothers and Morrison may have gotten into the illicit market, but the authorities definitely stopped 40 of them. Still, the three suspects were back on the street three months after the November encounter and were only arrested after the Zapata crime scene gun was traced back to Otilio.

The investigation revealed that Morrison had purchased at least 24 firearms from licensed dealers between July 10 and Nov. 4, 2010.

This case demonstrated that current laws – when enforced – do work. The ATF gun trace mechanism worked to quickly link the Zapata crime scene gun with the man who bought it.

Once that connection was made – as in the case of the gun that was found at the Brian Terry murder scene – ATF moved quickly to arrest the individual who bought the gun. But it was *only after* those guns were linked to the separate slayings of two federal law enforcement officers that swift arrests were made.

Earlier in this chapter, we quoted author Scott Stewart's piece for *Stratfor Global Intelligence*. He underscored the problem with this 90-percent figure when he noted, "It has now become quite common to hear U.S. officials confidently assert that 90 percent of the weapons used by the Mexican drug cartels come from the United States. However, a close examination of the dynamics of the cartel wars in Mexico — and of how the oft-echoed 90 percent number was reached — clearly demonstrates that the number is more political rhetoric than empirical fact."

Critics of the "Fast and Furious" program – including sources inside ATF – suggested both seriously and sarcastically that revelations about the number of firearms that ATF officials allowed to enter the black market may explain where a lot of those guns actually came from, and how traces so easily came back to gun shops in the Southwest.

To suggest that American gun laws and lazy gun dealers are to blame for violence in Mexico is even more ludicrous when one understands that during the Gunrunner investigation, several gun dealers reportedly voiced concerns about selling firearms to different suspects. Those retailers repeatedly raised apprehensions about customers who came into their shops with bags of cash to purchase firearms most closely associated with the weaponry commonly showing up in Mexico. Still, they were apparently told by ATF to allow the transactions to go through.

Imagine this scenario: Convenience store managers and employees in a certain community raise alarms about people who come into their stores to purchase large amounts of beer, wine and hard liquor. These concerned retailers are told by undercover officers or investigators to make the sales, even though they suspect the alcoholic beverages are being purchased for juveniles.

Then one night, a carload of drunken teens collides head-on with a police cruiser in another jurisdiction, and the officer is killed.

In retrospect, one could logically argue that firearms retailers were trying to do the job that law enforcement was *supposed* to be doing, but didn't. Instead, the retailers were essentially the fall guys or whipping boys in a sting operation that went horribly wrong.

Of course, none of these facts would ever matter to the gun prohibition lobby or its Congressional mouthpieces, because their agenda has never been about protecting the public from criminals, but only preventing or discouraging private firearms ownership.

But there is another aspect of this controversy that has clouded the debate for at least two decades. The so-called "assault weapons" that gun prohibitionists want banned because of the Mexican drug war – or whatever other *excuse du jour* they offer – are not real assault weapons at all, at least not the guns that were targeted by the Fast and Furious operation. These guns of U.S. origin are *semiautomatic look-alikes* of the military weapons. They function no differently than a duck hunter's semiautomatic shotgun. Their only crime is that they *look* different.

So there is no misunderstanding, the drug cartels definitely are in possession of fully-automatic assault weapons, plus rocket-propelled grenades and other anti-personnel ordnance, including light machine guns. However, the cartels are not obtaining any of that weaponry from American gun shops or gun shows, because those kinds of weapons are not sold in gun shops or at gun shows. To imply otherwise is a complete canard.

This takes us back to the gun tracing dilemma. The majority of firearms recovered from drug war crime scenes cannot be traced back to the United States because they come from other sources in Asia, South America, the Middle East or Europe. Yet, the American public is never widely apprised of this important fact because it does not fit with the gun prohibition agenda. There can be no other logical explanation for what amounts to a news blackout on this critical story element.

As Stewart revealed in his story for *Stratfor Global Intelligence*, military-grade firearms and other ordnance are "not generally available for sale" either in the U.S. or Mexico. He noted that a lot of these weapons come from China "via the same networks that furnish precursor chemicals for narcotics manufacturing."

"Latin America is awash in weapons that were shipped there over the past several decades to supply the various insurgencies and counterinsurgencies in the region," Stewart wrote. "When these military-grade weapons are combined with the rampant corruption in the region, they quickly find their way into the black arms market."

He further explained that such weapons of U.S. origin typically come from third-party sources rather than directly from the United States. Blaming so-called "lax" gun laws in the United States, once again, is an argument that is easily proven false, simply by looking at facts, as Stewart's article does.

Stewart's analysis was, of course, largely ignored, and certainly so by the mainstream press. It seems almost as though the press, which had seemingly made up its collective mind about the origins of guns in northern Mexico, decided that if details such as those brought to light by Stewart were ignored, they might just go away.

As it turns out, Stewart was not the first journalist to look behind the curtain, which translates to him not being the first journalist whose revelations were largely ignored by the three major networks.

As noted earlier in this chapter, the agency had refuted this 90-percent figure early in the controversy, but to little if any avail. Once that mythical "90 percent" became part of the nightly news lexicon, it was virtually impossible to correct the damage, even though Lajeunesse evidently had his facts solid.

According to his report, "In 2007-2008, according to ATF Special Agent William Newell, Mexico submitted 11,000 guns to the ATF for tracing. Close to 6,000 were successfully traced -- and of those, 90 percent -- 5,114 to be exact, according to testimony in Congress by William Hoover -- were found to have come from the U.S."

And this probably explains where the 90 percent figure came from. As Lajeunesse and Stewart, and a handful of other reporters tried to clarify, it was bogus.

Fox News' April 2009 report essentially demolished the assertion that American guns and the nation's lax gun laws were fueling the violence south of the border. The Fox report might be considered a precursor to Stewart's more detailed analysis, yet outside of the firearms community, they got very little attention.

During the years 2007-2008 noted above, the Mexican government reported seizing 29,000 firearms at various crime scenes in northern Mexico. The 11,000 guns alluded to earlier amounted to 32 percent of that total figure. According to Lajeunesse, "In other words, 68 percent of the guns that were recovered were never submitted for tracing. And when you weed out the roughly 6,000 guns that could not be traced from the remaining 32 percent, it means 83 percent of the guns found at crime scenes in Mexico could not be traced to the U.S."

Now would be a good time to wonder why, with all of this verifiable data available, the Obama administration and others have not simply corrected their earlier assertions.

Here's one possible explanation: It was dramatic, and that was exactly what the three large networks, and other press cheerleaders of the Obama administration seemed to want, even if it was erroneous. The administration does not care to admit it was wrong, and administration cheerleaders had no interest in putting the president on the spot by challenging the "legend that had become fact."

Here's another potential explanation: Providing the facts about this gun trafficking would not advance the anti-gun agenda, which includes – as noted earlier in this chapter – imposing hopelessly restrictive regulations on gun show operators and renewing, and making permanent, the ban on semiautomatic sport-utility rifles, which was considered a piece of trophy legislation by the gun prohibition lobby. They fought hard to keep that ban alive in 2004, but it was allowed to expire. They desperately want to revive it; to "condition" the American public to the notion that banning an entire class of firearms is acceptable.

Perhaps the best explanation came from Chris Cox, chief lobbyist for the National Rifle Association.

"Reporter after politician after news anchor just disregards the truth on this," Cox told Lajeunesse. "The numbers are intentionally used to weaken the Second Amendment."

Later in the Lajeunesse report, a comment from gun prohibitionist Tom Diaz, senior policy analyst at the

Violence Policy Center, put the issue in perspective. He said the 90 percent issue was a "red herring" that should not detract from the government's effort to stop gun trafficking, which, as the Project Gunrunner scandal appeared to reveal, had been somewhat enabled by the ATF.

Diaz reinforced the myth: "We know that one hell of a lot of firearms come from the United States because our gun market is wide open."

Except that, maybe, it is not…without some apparent, albeit careless or negligent, as Sen. Grassley suggested, help from the very agency whose job it is to interdict illegal gun trafficking.

Six

GUN SAFETY LAWS
SAVE CHILDREN

Q. *Why shouldn't American gun owners support gun safety laws that protect families and children?*

Following the devastating 1994 Congressional elections that saw Democrats lose control of Capitol Hill largely due to their pro-gun control votes on the 1993 Brady Law and 1994 Clinton ban on semiautomatic rifles and full-capacity magazines, gun prohibitionists realized they needed to re-package their message and their image.

With pro-gun Republicans in charge, anti-gunners at the Brady Center to Prevent Gun Violence – formerly Handgun Control, Inc. – and the Violence Policy Center concluded that the term "gun control" was political poison. They could no longer afford, politically or financially, to talk about gun "control."

Thus was born the "gun safety" movement. The agenda remained the same, but it was carefully presented with new packaging designed to be more appealing to a larger audience. A cooperative press was all too willing to adopt the new term in reporting the firearms issue.

Jennifer Freeman with the pro-gun Liberty Belles group discussed this chameleon change by anti-gunners in a short essay headlined "Old Tricks, New Phrases, Same Agenda." She detailed how the gun ban movement became the "gun control" movement and eventually morphed into the "gun safety" movement "By employing a variety of innocuous terms designed to mislead, confuse, and lull the average American into a false sense of security..."

"In addition to 'gun safety'," she explained, "they have nearly eliminated the term 'ban' in favor of soundbite friendly words like: Sensible, safe, and common-sense. These words are appealing to the average American and are not likely to generate any resistance."

There was even a new organization to push gun control initiatives: Americans for Gun Safety. Who could argue with a title like that?

Actually, a lot of people could argue and did so, especially after they looked past the façade and discovered that AGS was bankrolled by the liberal, anti-gun Tides Center, a San Francisco-based non-profit that was dedicated to educating the public about gun laws and "new policy options for reducing access to guns by criminals and children and to promote responsible gun ownership," according to a short description on Wikipedia.

But the Tides Center and AGS were far more interested in discouraging gun ownership altogether than they were in promoting even what they called "responsible" gun ownership.

The AGS agenda was straight out of the gun control playbook, with a wish list that included background checks for all firearms transactions, including private transactions between even family members and personal friends. They also want such checks for all transactions, even between private parties, at gun shows, and to open mental health records to law enforcement access for the purpose of preventing people with mental health problems from legally purchasing guns. Mental health professionals have, in many cases, resisted this sort of intrusion as a violation of doctor-patient privacy.

Not long after AGS was founded, the National Rifle Association exposed the organization as essentially a front for gun control. The NRA wrote on its website:

> *No claim is too outrageous for the anti-gun lobbyists masquerading under the name "Americans for Gun Safety" (AGS). Unfortunately, much of the media is willing to play along with AGS`s deceptions, depicting the group as a "moderate voice," a "third way" in the gun-policy debate.*
>
> *For the record, AGS has nothing to do with gun safety. It is an organization whose sole founder, a former board member of Handgun Control, Inc., has a highly focused and barely hidden agenda: licensing all American gun owners and registering every firearm they own.*
>
> *AGS is staffed by the architects of the anti-gun schemes of Bill Clinton and Sen. Charles Schumer. Its president is Jonathan Cowan, who served at the right hand of the self-appointed anti-gun Czar of the Clinton cabinet--HUD Secretary Andrew Cuomo, whose agenda for fighting crime revolved around threatening nonsensical lawsuits against gun makers. Cowan is assisted by Clinton White House political aide Matt Bennett, and by Jim Kessler, the former gun-control advisor to Senator Charles Schumer.*
>
> *These credentials may explain the insistence of AGS in perpetrating clear falsehoods. The previous Administration championed the tactic of "tell a lie often enough, and soon it becomes the truth." AGS is clearly hoping that the same tactic will prevail in its assault on gun shows.*

When it comes to practicing genuine gun safety, no organization more capably delivers that message – with certified instruction to back it up – than the NRA.

The association has a network of volunteer firearms instructors in all 50 states, and annually provides firearms instruction to millions of Americans. Among many

Americans, the NRA is known as "the Red Cross of firearms instruction."

By contrast, neither AGS, nor the Brady Center, nor the Violence Policy Center and their state-level affiliates offer any kind of firearms safety instruction. Their "gun safety" message is a mix of "guns are bad" and "most people are too stupid to have one in the house." They have no instructors who teach hands-on safe gun handling, nor do they have a history of instruction.

Indeed, the NRA has been teaching firearms safety and marksmanship for more than a century. It was the NRA – not some gun control organization – that spearheaded hunter education in the United States, starting with a program in New York State in 1949.

However, referring to gun control groups as "gun safety advocates" has become standard fare in the liberal lexicon. Even President Barack Obama used it in an opinion piece he wrote about gun control after the attempted assassination of Arizona Congresswoman Gabrielle Giffords. The article, which originally appeared in the *Arizona Daily Star* in Tucson – where the shooting occurred – included the following passage:

> *The fact is, almost all gun owners in America are highly responsible. They're our friends and neighbors. They buy their guns legally and use them safely, whether for hunting or target shooting, collection or protection. And that's something that gun-safety advocates need to accept. Likewise, advocates for gun owners should accept the awful reality that gun violence affects Americans everywhere, whether on the streets of Chicago or at a supermarket in Tucson.*

Author Gottlieb, chairman of the Citizens Committee for the Right to Keep and Bear Arms, responded accusing the president of equating gun control with gun safety "when in reality the self-proclaimed 'safety' advocates spend all of their time spreading anti-gun hysteria, and none of it promoting responsible gun ownership."

"The president evidently can't tell the difference between genuine gun safety advocates and gun prohibitionists," Gottlieb said.

He explained that true gun safety advocates "understand real gun safety involves muzzle control, proper storage, practiced marksmanship, and general safe handling. The so-called 'gun safety advocates' to whom the president alludes in his comments are prohibitionists who hide their true intentions behind a façade of pseudo-responsibility."

He blistered gun prohibitionists by noting that "Their idea of 'gun safety' is to make gun ownership prohibitively expensive by adopting registration and licensing fees, and regulations that are deliberately written to discourage average citizens from exercising their Second Amendment rights."

So-called "gun safety" laws that the gun prohibition lobby supports have little, if anything to even remotely do with actual child safety, but the sales pitch sounds better if one couches it with images of smiling children in danger of being shot dead in their homes or at school or a day care center. It is doubtful that straightforward acknowledgement of an agenda calling for licensing and registration, lengthy waiting periods, invasive background checks that include access to a person's confidential medical files from physicians and high fees from firearms owners to pay for all of that red tape would gain much traction with average American citizens.

So, they package the true gun control objectives as "child safety" measures.

About the closest these "gun safety" proposals come to actually offering some measure of protection for children would be proposed mandatory gun safety locks and mandatory safe storage requirements that are part of the typical agenda. However, in practice, both mandates have been abject failures wherever they have been imposed because the irresponsible people at whom such regulations are aimed are the very people who habitually ignore them.

Such laws are unenforceable. There are no "gun storage police" who can casually visit the home of a gun owner and, without benefit of a search warrant, stroll in and observe whether someone has his or her firearm safely stored. While some gun prohibitionists would be delighted to see such a requirement become law on a national scale, they would not dare say so publicly.

Most of these "gun safety" measures are aimed at adults and are proposed as effective steps toward disarming criminals and irresponsible people. In practice, such laws have been demonstrable failures. After the now-defunct handgun bans were adopted in Chicago and Washington, D.C., the violent crime and homicide in both cities escalated dramatically.

Legislation establishing "Gun Free School Zones" has yet to prevent a single school shooting. America has racked up quite a body count of students and their teachers that prove the ineffectiveness of such statutes. At the same time there have been numerous "Zero Tolerance" expulsions for such grievances as grade school children having tiny rubber guns from action figures, or doodling a picture of a firearm. In one case in Virginia, a student was expelled for wearing a T-shirt from a summer camp that depicted a competitive shooter, an action that resulted in a lawsuit filed against the school.

Legislation requiring background checks has been of dubious success, since anecdotal evidence suggests that thousands of people whose gun purchases were initially denied – yet whose denials become part of the statistics gun ban groups use to show how many "criminals" have been denied gun purchases thanks to the Brady law – eventually got their firearms after appealing the denials.

Laws limiting gun sales to one per month did not stop Sueng Hui Cho, the Virginia Tech gunman, nor have they stemmed the illicit flow of firearms to places like New York and Chicago. We will discuss this situation in greater detail in Chapter Twelve.

Waiting periods have not been successful in preventing "heat of passion" killings or suicides, and there is no way to prove otherwise. There is ample evidence that shows people who are determined to end their own lives will do so, even if a firearm is not available. There are also countless police reports of spousal or domestic partner homicides that involved stabbings, blunt instrument beatings, poisonings and strangling.

Perhaps the biggest stretch of credulity has been the attempt by gun prohibitionists to oppose concealed carry reform measures, and then pressure private businesses to prohibit legal concealed carry on their premises "for the safety of families and children."

Using the child safety argument to push gun control measures has been alternated with buzz word campaigns that sell restrictive gun laws as "common sense" or "reasonable" when they are neither. However, the strategy has been effective in that it telegraphs to people in the middle that opponents of such gun measures, no matter how extreme in nature, are "unreasonable" and they lack "common sense."

What is a "reasonable" gun law? That depends upon to whom one is listening at any given moment, and which organization he or she represents, and what is high on their agenda.

For some, it is "reasonable" to require licensing of gun owners and registration of all of their guns. For others, it is "common sense" to publicize the names of gun owners so that their neighbors have the opportunity to know who may have a firearm in a home where their child might visit.

A "sensible" gun law as envisioned by gun control advocates might require a gun owner to keep his or her firearm disassembled and/or locked up and unloaded. That was the case in Washington, D.C. until 2008 when the U.S. Supreme Court declared such a requirement to be nonsense in *Heller*.

There is one measure that is a trophy for gun prohibitionists, and that is a ban on semiautomatic sport-utility rifles. This was the focus of the Clinton ban of 1994-2004, and the gun ban lobby desperately wants that ban revived and made permanent. They have repeatedly demonstrated that they will attempt to exploit any tragedy to further that effort.

A good example of the typical agenda of a gun ban organization was offered by Ralph Fascitelli, president of Washington CeaseFire, a small but vocal group based in Seattle. Following a gang-related shooting that left one person dead at a popular state park in the Seattle suburb of Issaquah in 2010, Fascitelli offered the following solutions to such an incident:

> • *First let's ask our politicians in Olympia to ban guns in all state, county and city parks, where we have now seen more than once that a toxic combination of alcohol, firearms and elevated testosterone on a sunny day can have deadly consequences. Let's make our parks gun-free zones where families can gather with peace of mind without the worry of sudden death to innocent loved ones (and let's have our park rangers make spot checks to ensure that no one does indeed have a gun in their possession). State lawmakers can do this much easier than municipalities or county government due to the prevailing state law of pre-emption on gun legislation.*
> • *Second, let's close the gun-show loophole and insist on mandatory background checks on all gun purchases. More than one-fourth of juvenile crimes involve guns procured from gun shows, according to a survey by the Portland Police Department. Insisting that felons, the mentally ill and underage juveniles do not have easy access to handguns or military assault weapons is not an infringement on Second Amendment rights.*
> • *Finally, let's make it more difficult for people to get concealed-weapons permits or to openly carry loaded weapons. Currently there is no training, testing or registration required in procuring a concealed-weapons permit in this state, and no permit is required to openly carry a loaded weapon. Incredibly, it's legal to openly carry a loaded weapon*

*in government buildings at the state Capitol and, yes,
even at a Starbucks.*

Parks are public property for all citizens, even those
who choose to legally arm themselves, and who have
carried guns in parks for years without harming anyone.
The shooting Fascitelli was attempting to exploit involved
gang members or associates.

There is no evidence that any of the people involved
purchased or otherwise obtained any of their firearms
from a gun show. However, closing the so-called "gun show
loophole" is high on the gun control agenda, so proponents
of restrictive gun laws invariably toss that in as a solution
to some violent incident, even when the two are totally
unrelated.

Gun prohibitionists despise "shall issue" concealed
carry laws that require carry permits or licenses to be issued
to any law-abiding citizen who meets the qualifications,
which typically involve passing a background check. They
are equally contemptuous of Open Carry, and Fascitelli
personally has a bit of history regarding the practice.

A transplant from the Northeast, Fascitelli was
shocked in early 2010 when he attended a legislative hearing
in Washington's state capitol in Olympia. He was there to
support a statewide ban on so-called "assault weapons,"
but to his chagrin, several opponents of the legislation
were Open Carry activists who showed up armed.

A visibly alarmed Fascitelli was observed by several
of these activists approaching a Washington State Patrol
trooper assigned to the capitol security detail, demanding
to know if officers had checked the citizens' handguns
to see if they were loaded. He also wondered why their
firearms were not simply prohibited in state government
buildings.

He was not happy when the trooper explained that
Open Carry and carrying firearms on the capitol campus
are perfectly legal practices under state law and the
state constitution. In Washington, there is no statutory
prohibition against peaceably open carrying of firearms,

therefore it is legal. There were a couple of hundred people at the hearing, and only one of them felt threatened or intimidated or unsafe: Ralph Fascitelli.

His displeasure continued later in the spring when Washington CeaseFire joined with the Brady Center in an attempt to bully and browbeat Starbucks Coffee into banning armed citizens in its shops. Seattle is the Starbucks headquarters city, and the coffee giant's response to this campaign was to simply explain that Starbucks follows existing state laws. The "ban-by-proxy" effort fell flat.

Washington resident gun owners quickly began referring to Fascitelli with sarcasm: "He ain't from around here."

It is because of the extremist attitudes of gun prohibition groups that the *Washington Times* could justifiably publish an editorial declaring that "The left has permanently lost the argument on gun control."

The editorial ran down a list of strong pro-gun-rights legislation that had been passed into law or was being considered by state legislatures.

"Despite their best efforts to take advantage of the tragic shooting in Arizona (of Rep. Gabrielle Giffords)," the *Washington Times* observed, "to promote pointless restrictions on things like the size of handgun magazines, the propaganda campaign is unlikely to go anywhere. Instead, the right to keep and bear arms continues to gain steam as state lawmakers around the country are enacting measures that would have been unthinkable not so long ago."

Among such measures would be open or concealed carry without a permit in Wyoming, Arizona and Alaska. They would include adoption of so-called "Castle Doctrine" statutes that, in actuality, are "Stand Your Ground" laws, meaning that law-abiding citizens who are attacked in their homes or in any other place where they have a right to be no longer have a duty to retreat before defending themselves.

The newspaper reminded its readers, "Whenever the left is defeated at the statehouse and ballot box, it turns to the courts. The Supreme Court shot down most of these efforts with the *District of Columbia v. Heller* and *McDonald v. City of Chicago* rulings reviving judicial recognition of the Second Amendment."

Many states have adopted laws that prohibit liability lawsuits against firearm and ammunition manufacturers. Other laws forbid local governments from adopting "emergency ordinances" that allow confiscation of firearms from citizens in case of a natural or man-made disaster.

And what about the children?

Oh, yes, the children; whenever the gun prohibition lobby is desperate for an argument to justify whatever it is they are after, or to deflect public attention away from an issue on which they are the losing side, they trot out "the children." Who, after all, could seriously advocate in favor of endangering children, or argue against laws that would make children safer?

According to data from the Centers for Disease and Control, and National Center for Injury Prevention and Control, fewer than 100 children below the age of 15 die annually as a result of firearms accidents. In the 15-24 age category, fewer than 200 unintentional firearms deaths are recorded annually.

That pales in comparison to the numbers killed in motor vehicle accidents, and comes in well behind the number of young people who drown.

But we should put something in perspective right here. In order to boost their numbers to make their arguments seem more pressing, gun control proponents will frequently include data from the young adult age group when discussing children.

Note the following from the Leitchfield, Kentucky Pediatric Clinic's website: "The American Academy of Pediatrics issued a statement this month reaffirming their longstanding position on gun control. They would like to see handguns and semiautomatic assault weapons banned and a much stricter regulation of the manufacture, sale, purchase, ownership, and use of all firearms. The rationale for this position is that firearm related deaths are at such a high level that this is a public health problem. In 1997, 32436 deaths resulted from firearms, including 4223 deaths in children under 20."

Children under...20? Who, other than a person laboring to pad the numbers, would consider a 20-year-old, or anybody age 19 or 18, to be a child, or even an adolescent?

Here's how the NRA looks at this sort of statistical chicanery: "Gun control supporters claim that firearm accidents take the lives of a dozen or more children daily, or 5,000 yearly, or one every 90 seconds. The Handgun Epidemic Lowering Plan (HELP) Network (dedicated to "changing society's attitude toward guns so that it becomes socially unacceptable for private citizens to have handguns") put the figure at nine per day. Some gun control supporters count anyone under age 24 as a "child," to get even higher numbers, by adding the relatively small number among children to the much larger number among juveniles and teenage adults, and calling the total "children." In fact, on average there is one such death among children per day, including one accidental death every seven days."

Perhaps Dr. Edgar A. Suter, chairman of Doctors for Integrity in Research & Public Policy, put this argument in its proper perspective when he wrote that "Prohibitionists foster the image of gun deaths of 'thousands of innocent children'."

"In order to make this claim," Dr. Suter observed, "they have had to include young adults (to age 24) involved in gang and drug crime - hardly 'innocent children.' 10 to 20 times more children die from car and other leading causes of accidental deaths as die from guns - for example, in 1988, compared with 2,608 car, 1,014 drowning, and 10,094 burn deaths, 123 children (ages 0-10) died from gun accidents."

Certainly, the death of any innocent child is a tragedy, and we should do everything humanly possible to reduce the numbers, especially since there are several organizations that are more than willing to artificially inflate those numbers. Gun prohibitionists would have the public believe that firearms civil rights advocates are casually willing to sacrifice children on the altar of gun rights, a notion that is preposterous.

Also on its website, the Leitchfield clinic alluded to a discredited study from the mid-1980s that claimed "Guns are 43 times more likely to kill someone who is known to the family than to kill an intruder." This questionable statistic is frequently used, even now, years after it has been picked apart by various researchers, to discourage people – especially young parents – from having firearms in their homes.

Dr. Suter also refuted this extraordinary claim, detailing how it started.

"In a 1985 article in the *New England Journal of Medicine*," he recalled, "Drs. (Arthur L.) Kellermann and (Donald T.) Reay described the proper way to calculate how many people are saved by guns compared to how many are hurt by guns. The benefits should include, in the authors' own words, 'cases in which burglars or intruders are wounded or frightened away by the use or display of a firearm [and] cases in which would-be intruders may have purposely avoided a house known to be armed...'

"However," Dr. Suter continued, "when Kellerman and Reay calculated their comparison, they did NOT include those cases, they only counted the times a homeowner KILLED the criminal. Because only 0.1% (1 in a 1,000) of defensive gun usage involves the death of the criminal, KELLERMANN AND REAY UNDERSTATED THE PROTECTIVE BENEFITS OF FIREARMS BY A FACTOR OF 1,000! They turned the truth on its head! Why? Kellermann emotionally confessed his anti-gun prejudice at the 1993 HELP Conference."

(Note: Kellermann later insisted that he never made any such admission. In a column written for the *Medical Sentinel* by editor-in-chief Dr. Miguel Faria, MD, he noted, "it was reported that during his formal presentation at the (October 17, 1993) HELP conference, in an emotional moment admitted his personal anti-gun bias (a bias that, as we have seen, is evident in the pattern of his research).")

"Although in a letter to the *Journal of the Medical Association of Georgia,*" Dr. Faria wrote, "Kellermann denied making such a statement at that specific meeting, he did not actually repudiate his general anti-gun bias.)

"Honest analysis," Suter explained, "even by Kellermann and Reay's own standards, shows the '43 times' comparison to be superficially appealing, but actually a deceitful contrivance -- unfortunately, a lie that is parroted by the well-funded gun-prohibition lobby and by gullible and biased journalists."

Kellermann, it should be noted, was an early advocate of the philosophy that firearms injuries are a public health issue. According to a brief biography of Dr. Kellermann on Wikipedia, his allegedly biased research so infuriated Republicans on Capitol Hill that in June 1996, the House Appropriations Committee – then under Republican control – stripped $2.6 million from the budget of the National Center for Injury Prevention and Control. This was, Wikipedia noted, "the exact amount previously set aside for NCIPC/CDC research into the causes and effects of firearm-related death and injury."

If preventing firearms mishaps among youngsters was foremost in the minds of gun control proponents, they would be lobbying school boards and state legislatures to mandate firearms safety training as part of the public school curriculum. According to the NRA, education decreases firearm accidents, and they have raw data and experience to back that up.

According to the NRA's website, "Youngsters learn firearm safety in NRA programs offered through civic groups such as the Boy Scouts, Jaycees, and American Legion, and schools. NRA's Eddie Eagle GunSafe program teaches children pre-K through 3rd grade that if they see a gun without supervision, they should 'STOP! Don't Touch. Leave The Area. Tell An Adult.' Since 1988, Eddie has been used by 26,000 schools, civic groups, and law enforcement agencies to reach more than 22 million children."

The award-winning Eddie Eagle program has been tremendously successful in spreading a neutral firearm safety message to youngsters across America. The other programs, including Boy Scouts and Jaycees, have provided hands-on instruction and experience to youngsters and teens in several states.

Meanwhile, anti-gunners have continued pushing their prohibitionist agenda, which promotes ignorance and fear of firearms, rather than working knowledge and healthy respect. Likewise, they use every opportunity to advance that agenda, even through subtle reinforcement.

Again, quoting the Leitchfield clinic's website: "Let your legislators know about your feelings about gun safety. There are a number of non-controversial issues that can protect our children and not infringe on gun ownership rights. Assault weapons have no purpose other than killing people, and should be banned. Trigger locks and other safety measures should be required. Push for stricter enforcement of the existing laws. Crimes committed with guns should be punished to the fullest extent of the law. Gun toting criminals need to be off the street."

This is political rhetoric, not pediatrics, especially that sentence about banning so-called "assault weapons." Childhood firearm fatalities that involve such firearms, which have been called "modern sporting rifles" by the National Shooting Sports Foundation, are so infrequent as to be almost non-existent. However, including this plea to parents is an example of how the gun prohibition message is inserted into places where it does not belong.

Americans do support measures that provide a layer of safety for families and children, but the gun control initiatives repeatedly put forth by the prohibition lobby do not accomplish that, and never have.

Seven

ACCESS TO GUNS
IS FAR TOO EASY

Q. *What is wrong with laws that are designed to prevent easy access to guns?*

Beginning with the infamous "Black Codes" of the post-Civil War South, there have been a string of gun laws adopted at the local, state and even federal level that increasingly placed restrictions on a citizen's right to keep and bear arms.

The Black Codes were adopted by racist Southerners, led primarily by Democrats whose singular goal was to prevent freed blacks from enjoying the rights of citizenship, including owning or possessing firearms with which they might defend themselves from attack by night riders, typified by the Ku Klux Klan.

Another type of gun law was adopted in New York by the Tammany Hall political machine to prevent immigrants from southern Europe as a means of keeping them disarmed during that era. New York adopted the "Sullivan Law" in 1911, requiring people to obtain a license to possess a handgun even in one's own home. As noted by author

William R. Tonso in his excellent treatise on the Sullivan Act called *Gun Control: White Man's Law*, "For instance, when the Sullivan Law was enacted, southern and eastern European immigrants were considered racially inferior and religiously and ideologically suspect. (Many were Catholics or Jews, and a disproportionate number were anarchists or socialists.)." This remains one of the most restrictive gun control laws in the nation and countless numbers of New York residents have been prosecuted for violating this law.

In the West, local ordinances that prohibited the carrying of firearms in towns like Dodge City and Tombstone were adopted ostensibly to prevent drunken cowboys from shooting up the town. However, such laws also made it easier for local lawmen, such as Wyatt Earp and Bat Masterson, to manhandle the drunks. It was one of the contributing factors for the famous "Gunfight at the OK Corral," between the Earp brothers and a rival faction involving the Clanton and McLaury brothers, as many citizens of that silver mining boomtown were reluctant to surrender their firearms as a condition of remaining in town and going about their business.

The rivalry was largely political in nature, though historians have detailed the conflict as also involving the illegal activities of the larger Clanton faction, identified as the cowboys. Cattle rustling, horse stealing, stage robbery and other crimes have been attributed to members of that faction, but the disarmament of Tombstone citizens only served to exacerbate an already temperamental situation.

One might observe that the municipal gun ban in Tombstone did not prevent that famous gun battle, but may actually have been the catalyst.

If one were to analyze such laws, they have always been about power; who has it and who doesn't.

Over the years, as the gun prohibition movement gathered momentum (this effort has never been about gun "control" or gun "safety" but about prohibiting as many people as possible from owning or possessing firearms), their various schemes have always been pandered as "good first steps" toward fighting crime and protecting communities. When the term "gun control" became politically toxic, the prohibition lobby simply played with semantics and became the "gun safety" movement. Of course, their operative term had nothing to do with genuine firearms safety, but with their peculiar definition of safety, which translated to prohibiting average citizens from owning and using firearms.

But the term "gun safety" strikes a far less ominous chord with the American public than does the term "gun control" and it sounds oh-so-reasonable. The underlying agenda is still the same, carefully repackaged with new buzz words, and the ultimate goal remains unchanged: Prohibition or prohibitively strict regulation of private firearms ownership that discourages people from having firearms or wanting to buy them, or simply prohibits such a purchase for any number of reasons.

There has been a long-standing argument that crime was less frequent in the days when people could purchase firearms without background checks or waiting periods. Anecdotal accounts of people solving their domestic problems by running down to the corner gun store and coming back home an hour later to murder their spouse seemed to sound pretty much the same, almost as though they were based on the same incident, told and re-told as though each re-telling was a separate case. In the end, those stories may largely end up in the "urban myth" category, but they were politically useful at the time for convincing the public, and especially state and local lawmakers, that "something needed to be done" to stem the violence.

Likewise, the liberal press and the gun prohibition lobby capitalized on tragic incidents including the assassinations of John and Robert Kennedy and Dr. Martin Luther King to pressure Capitol Hill's passage of the 1968 Gun Control Act. This law placed considerable restrictions on the ability of law-abiding citizens to purchase firearms, particularly when coupled with state-level regulations.

In the final analysis, there is no such thing today as "easy access to guns." At least, access is not so easy for law-abiding citizens who legally purchase firearms from federally-licensed firearms dealers. Guns remain readily available to the criminal element. They merely need to steal firearms, often from police officers, or obtain them via other means, through "straw purchase" by another party, or from relatives, friends or street acquaintances.

But for average citizens of good standing, buying a gun is an experience that has attached to it varying degrees of inconvenience, depending upon one's state or even city of residence.

For all citizens purchasing firearms from a licensed retailer, there is the mandatory federal background check, making the Second Amendment the only constitutional civil right that, in order to exercise it, one must first get permission from a federal law enforcement agency. Try attaching that standard to the exercise of the First Amendment and the nation's newspapers; broadcasters and on-line journalists would howl.

There is a considerable amount of hypocrisy on the part of the mainstream press when it comes to exercising and protecting civil rights. The press is aggressively protective of the First Amendment right of free speech and a free press, but largely supportive of broad restrictions on the Second Amendment right to keep and bear arms. Both are individual civil rights delineated and protected by the Bill of Rights.

Editorials are abundant that exclaim guns are far too accessible, yet the adoption of regulation upon regulation, restrictive statutes followed by more statutes – all of which have essentially penalized the law-abiding citizens for crimes they did not commit – have not prevented criminals from getting all the firepower they seem to desire.

As Prof. Gary Mauser, a veteran gun rights researcher based in Canada, has noted, "The introduction of stricter firearms regulations is almost always justified as a reaction to a recent rise in violent crime, although fears of political unrest may be equally important if less often discussed publicly. Politicians promise that restrictive gun laws will make society safer, but proof has been lacking. Such laws must be demonstrated to cut violent crime, homicide and suicide, or these claims are hollow promises. It's time to ask if stringent gun laws actually work because regardless of how restrictive such laws are, and the trend is to be ever more restrictive, these kinds of laws impose high costs on citizens by stimulating the growth of governmental bureaucracy."

Mauser reported in a paper titled *"Do Restrictive Firearm Laws Improve Public Safety?"* that "Empirical support for firearms laws has proved to be elusive in the U.S. as well as the UK." He cited research released by the U.S. National Academy of Sciences that had reviewed more than 250 journal articles, 99 books and more than 40 government publications, yet it "could not identify any gun law that had reduced violent crime, suicide or gun accidents." One year earlier, Mauser added, the Centers for Disease Control had come to "a similar conclusion."

He focused on one such regulation that had been promulgated across the landscape, and adopted into law, the so-called "gun-free zone."

"The...mass shootings at Virginia Tech vividly illustrate the failure of restrictive gun laws to protect the public," Mauser observed. "Virginia Tech, like almost all schools, is a 'gun free zone.' Obviously, gun bans do not keep murderers from obtaining or using guns."

Prof. Mauser added: "The crucial test is whether gun laws improve public safety. There is no social benefit in restricting the availability of guns if total murder and suicide rates remain unchanged. It is difficult to claim that public safety is better if there is no decrease in the number of lives lost. The evidence...indicates that all that is accomplished (at best) by the removal of one particular means is that people manage to kill themselves or others by some other means."

This falls on deaf ears in the gun prohibition camp, where people like Paul Helmke, former president of the Brady Center to Prevent Gun Violence, repeatedly laments about the "all-too easy access to guns." Easy, perhaps, for criminals, but hardly for the law-abiding citizens who wish to arm themselves for defense against these same criminals.

Helmke and other anti-gunners quickly capitalized on the January 2011 attempted assassination of Arizona Congresswoman Gabrielle Giffords – an incident that left six people dead and thirteen wounded – to push for more gun restrictions while complaining loudly that there were "loopholes" that allowed the gunman, Jared Lee Loughner, to legally purchase the pistol used in that crime. This happened despite Loughner's history of erratic behavior that got him thrown out of a community college, and the fact that local authorities were familiar with him.

Yet, when Helmke complained in an opinion piece written for *Opposing Views* in the wake of the Giffords shooting, he inadvertently admitted that gun control efforts failed to prevent the attack. Helmke's opening statement read, "What America has been doing to prevent gun violence isn't working."

What Mr. Helmke carefully did not mention is that what America has been doing to prevent gun violence has involved enforcing laws that his organization and other like-minded groups insisted be enacted to prevent gun violence. So, when he complained that the measures taken to prevent such incidents were not working, he was actually criticizing the very laws that his organization had fought for.

Congress adopted the Brady Law requiring background checks. Jared Lee Loughner passed that check, and so did Virginia Tech gunman Seung Hui-Cho. So did Naveed Afzal Haq, the self-styled terrorist who shot six women, one of them fatally, at the Seattle Jewish Federation office in July 2006. But the Brady camp has a quick "out" for those crimes: The authorities did not do enough to identify these people. Now the gun prohibition lobby wants to expand and intensify the invasive nature of background checks, and allow the government to reach out and obtain someone's medical and mental health files.

Helmke's throw-away line is used almost by reflex anymore: "It's not enough." It is never enough. There are never enough hoops through which someone can jump to finally buy a firearm and exercise a fundamental civil right.

Where are the Helmkes of the world when someone with a history of drunken driving violations buys a new car and a month later, kills a family or a carload of college students, or a young father with a young family, or a single mother on her way home from a second job she has just to make ends meet? Do they come out of the woodwork with attacks on the car company, or the car dealer who sold the car?

That Helmke and Mauser are polar opposites in their view of the dilemma is understandable. Helmke, before taking over as head of the Brady Campaign, was a three-term mayor of Fort Wayne, Indiana, and an unsuccessful candidate for the U.S. Senate from that state. He attended Indiana University and Yale Law School at the same time as Bill and Hillary Clinton, and knew them both, according to his Wikipedia biography. He got involved in politics in high school.

Mauser is *Professor Emeritus* at the faculty of Business Administration and the Institute for Urban Canadian Research Studies at Simon Fraser University in Burnaby, British Columbia. He has a Ph.D. from the University of California at Irvine, and he has dual citizenship in Canada and the United States. For more than 15 years, Prof. Mauser has "conducted research on the politics of gun control, the effectiveness of gun control laws, and the use of firearms in self-defense."

One is a politician, the other an academic. The reader may judge which of them has the better motives.

While this can hardly be brought down to the level of a fundamental philosophical disagreement between two men, the argument over gun control laws quite often is just that, a philosophical disagreement. Gun prohibitionists battle more on the emotional level while gun rights advocates more typically take an analytical approach.

Proof of that can be found in the assertion that started this chapter, that access to guns is "too easy." Depending upon your state or local gun laws, legally obtaining a firearm, especially a handgun for personal protection, can be quite difficult and time consuming, and in some cases, expensive, thus rendering the argument preposterous that access to guns is too easy.

In April 2011, the City of New York and Mayor Michael Bloomberg were sued in federal district court by the Second Amendment Foundation, New York State Rifle & Pistol Association and seven private citizens over the fees that the city was charging simply to obtain a "premises permit." That is, a permit to have a handgun in one's own home, or place of business. This permit does not all a handgun to be carried on the street.

The premises permit fee was $340, making it cost-prohibitive from the outset for an average family budget. On top of that, the city also charged $94.25 for fingerprinting at the time of application for the permit. The application process could take several months, and if the premises permit is approved, it must be renewed every three years for another $340.

Anywhere in New York State, in order to even possess a firearm, one must have a permit. The cost of such permits outside New York City is a fraction of what the city charges.

In Illinois, private citizens must have a Firearm Owner's Identification (FOID) Card in order to legally possess any kind of firearm, although in early 2011, the Illinois State Supreme Court ruled that people permitted to carry guns in other states can transport them in Illinois without an Illinois FOID. However, because the state has prohibitions against concealed and open carry of firearms for personal protection, the Second Amendment Foundation filed a federal lawsuit against this prohibition. They were joined by Illinois Carry and two private citizens.

In New Jersey, citizens must apply for a firearms purchaser identification card before they are allowed to buy a gun. Each applicant must "provide the names and addresses of two reputable citizens personally acquainted with him as references." In the Garden State, officials empowered to grant or deny carry permit applications routinely reject those applications. The Second Amendment Foundation filed a federal lawsuit against New Jersey officials for deprivation of civil rights under color of law. They were joined in the action by the Association of New Jersey Rifle and Pistol Clubs and several private citizens.

In Maryland, the permitting process is much the same, with officials there having the authority to arbitrarily deny an application or a renewal because the applicant cannot provide "good cause" to be issued a permit. The Second Amendment Foundation filed a federal lawsuit on behalf of a Maryland resident whose permit renewal was rejected because he could not demonstrate a need or an "apprehended danger." This, despite the fact that a man he held at gunpoint a few years earlier, and who had been imprisoned for attacking the plaintiff in his home, is now back out on the streets and living within a couple of miles of the plaintiff.

California requires registration of handguns. People who move to the state have 60 days in which to register their handguns. Any kind of a firearm transfer must go through a licensed firearms dealer. Wikipedia says California has some of the most complex gun laws in the nation.

In all four states mentioned above, some of the highest crime rates are annually recorded.

Unfortunately, when restrictive gun laws are proven to have failed in their advertised mission of reducing crime, gun control proponents are loath to acknowledge their laws don't work. Instead, they argue that the laws were not strong enough, so a new and more restrictive law is invariably their answer. The gun prohibition movement has skillfully used this piecemeal strategy over the years to continually erode gun rights, while remaining essentially unable to provide verifiable statistics on how any of their proposals resulted in lower crime rates.

In recent years, however, public sentiment has been drifting away from the philosophy of increased restrictions, and instead focused on enforcement of existing laws.

This leaves gun prohibitionists such as Helmke defending polling data like that of one survey in Indiana that revealed more support for leaving gun laws alone than for making laws stricter. Helmke and his organization have spent recent years campaigning to preserve the laws they pushed for years, rather than see them eroded by such measures as liberalized concealed carry or expansion of so-called "castle doctrine" laws more accurately are described as "stand your ground" statutes. Such laws strengthen self-defense rights away from a person's home or place of business, and cover citizens who defend themselves against attack in public areas.

The pendulum has been swinging back from the extremist positions once successfully pandered by Helmke and/or his contemporaries in the gun prohibition movement, and part of the reason can be found earlier in this chapter. Capitalizing on tragedies such as the Giffords' shooting in Tucson has lost its appeal to a majority of Americans, not because they have become callous to violent crime and human suffering, but perhaps because they have recognized that these crimes are continuing, despite promises and predictions to the contrary.

Laws adopted on the promise that they would prevent violent crime have not lived up to their advertising, and the public has seen that. While people may not be so eager to repeal such laws, they are in no great hurry to expand them, either.

Part of this may be due to the Supreme Court rulings on Second Amendment rights, that first affirmed the right to keep and bear arms is an individual right, and that this right extends to all citizens in every state. Nearly all of the harshest gun control laws were adopted prior to the Supreme Court's 2008 *Heller* ruling that the Second Amendment protects an individual right. Henceforth, lawmakers will be more careful to craft statutes that place some limits on the exercise of that right.

Where does this leave the gun prohibition movement? Perhaps it puts anti-gunners in the uncomfortable position in which American gun owners found themselves for so many years: Defending what they have now against legislative and judicial erosion.

Yet, what they have may be of debatable worth, since there is no incontrovertible evidence that the gun laws promoted and adopted during the era of successful gun control lobbying ever prevented a single violent crime. Indeed, data from Chicago and Washington, D.C. shows that violent crime actually increased in the years after both cities adopted their now-defunct handgun bans.

In reporting his study results in *Do Restrictive Firearm Laws Improve Public Safety,"* Prof. Mauser did not limit his observations to the United States. Instead, he cited data from other countries that have adopted the kinds of gun control laws that American anti-gunners have promoted. Turning to the United Kingdom's gun laws adopted since the 1996 Dunblane massacre in Scotland, Mauser looked at the crime data and came to this conclusion: "Clearly, there is no evidence that firearm laws have caused homicide or violent crime to fall. *The firearm laws may even have increased criminal violence by disarming the general public* (emphasis added)."

"This review of violent crime trends in the United Kingdom, Australia and Canada," Mauser observed, "found that in the years following the introduction of British-style gun laws, despite massive increases in governmental bureaucracy, total homicide rates either increased or remained stable. Similar trends were observed in total violent crime. Importantly, in not one of these countries did the new gun laws appear to result in a decrease in total homicide rates despite the enormous costs to taxpayers. The situation is even clearer in the Republic of Ireland and Jamaica where violent crime, particularly murder, became much worse after the bans in both countries. Clearly, the factors driving the increasing rates of violent crime, e.g., organized crime or terrorism, were not curtailed by British style gun laws."

Ultimately, Mauser noted at the conclusion of his paper that, "this study corroborates American research that has been unable to identify any gun law that had reduced violent crime, suicide or gun accidents (Hahn *et al* 2003; Wellford 2004)."

As would any researcher devoted to digging out the facts, Mauser acknowledged that academics and other researchers would probably need to wait for data from other countries "to determine which elements are the most effective in reducing crime: aggressive police activity, increasing prison populations, capital punishment or empowering citizens to defend themselves."

"Nevertheless," Mauser wrote, "the failure of British-style gun laws in all of the countries examined here should give pause to anyone who imagines that efforts to impose international controls on firearms will be successful in reducing criminal or political violence."

Mauser's remarks should serve as an alarm against anyone posturing for additional gun controls because the ones already in place have not accomplished what was promised, or at the very least, implied by those who pushed such measures into law.

But let us look at the so-called "easy access" complaint.

As history has repeatedly demonstrated, restrictive gun laws do not prevent criminals from obtaining firearms, whether through direct action such as theft from homes, cars or firearms-related businesses, or indirect means that may include acquisition from acquaintances, friends or relatives. Guns are available on the streets for sale or as barter for drugs or other items. Firearms are also obtained from police, typically via theft from police vehicles.

Perhaps the most infamous of such thefts involved a single handgun stolen from the parked car belonging to then Seattle Police Chief Gil Kerlikowske. He left that position for a job as the Obama administration's "Drug Czar," but the story of the theft followed him.

During his tenure as police chief, Kerlikowske appeared before the Washington Legislature to lobby in support of tougher gun laws in the Evergreen State. Occasionally, he would speak on the same panels as representatives from Washington CeaseFire.

On Dec. 26, 2004, Kerlikowske took his wife downtown for some post-holiday shopping. He left his personally-owned Glock 9mm pistol in the car, which he said was locked, although investigators apparently could find no evidence of a forcible break-in. The gun was gone and has never been recovered.

Other law enforcement agencies have lost guns, including fully-automatic firearms from SWAT vehicles. Nobody has been immune. Federal agents with various agencies, state police, sheriff's deputies and local police have all been sources of illicit firearms. Some of those guns have subsequently been recovered at crime scenes.

The United States is abundant with firearms, and it would be impossible to prevent at least some of those guns from falling into the wrong hands. Suggesting otherwise is ludicrous, and arguing that safe storage laws, or one-gun-a-month regulations, or any other statutory limitation will provide a panacea to firearms theft or illicit gun trading that contributes to violent crime amounts to wishful thinking. The most Draconian of these laws are measures that punish gun owners for losing their guns to criminals. This kind of law victimizes the gun owner twice, once at the hands of the criminal, and then again at the hands of the government. Of course, proponents of such measures consider them a deterrent, not merely to crime, but to citizens who are thinking about owning a firearm. The more people they can deter from buying guns lawfully, the better prohibitionists like it.

So the dilemma remains; criminals can obtain firearms despite every well meaning, and not-so-well-meaning effort to prevent it. This so-called "easy access" to guns is something of a straw man argument, sometimes in a literal sense. It shifts public focus away from government's failure to prevent crime even after the adoption of so many federal, state and local laws and ordinances ostensibly designed to do just that, and places law-abiding gun owners under additional scrutiny merely for exercising a civil right.

What this scenario demonstrates time and again is that it is far easier to deflect public attention and point fingers of blame at gun owners than it is to actually provide workable solutions to violent crime. As the nation saw in 2009 when the violent drug wars in northern Mexico erupted in earnest, the Obama administration was quick to affix blame to gun shops and gun shows in the United States, and gun laws that enable private citizens to own semi-automatic modern sport-utility rifles that merely resemble military firearms. It became quickly apparent that the Obama administration was merely using the violence south of the border as an opportunity to float trial balloons about the possible renewal of a ban on so-called "assault weapons," and this time, make it permanent.

Two years later, following the exposure of the Project Gunrunner fiasco operated by the Bureau of Alcohol, Tobacco, Firearms and Explosives that was discussed in Chapter Five, there was a sense of *karma* because of revelations that the agency had allowed hundreds, if not thousands of firearms to be moved into the illegal traffic pipeline to Mexico. It becomes remarkably easy for criminals to obtain firearms when a federal "sting" operation actually allows it to happen.

As noted in our Chapter Five discussion, Senator Charles Grassley of Iowa launched an investigation. So did California Congressman Darrell Issa, chairman of the House Committee on Oversight and Government Reform. There is no need to repeat the details here, as we will discuss this controversy in greater detail in Chapter Eleven.

On the subject of straw men, it must be acknowledged that so-called "straw man" gun purchases – that is, transactions conducted by someone with a clean record who funnels legally-purchased guns to illegal recipients – do provide guns to the illicit market. Such transactions are often difficult to spot, unless they are conducted repeatedly at the same location by the same individuals. While that was the case with the Project Gunrunner effort and its subsidiary, Operation Fast and Furious, many times the straw purchases are occasional or even one-time-only affairs.

The "straw man" may actually be a woman buying a gun for a boyfriend or spouse, filling out the required paperwork and going through the required background check. Their records are clean, so they pass the check.

While this may fall within the "easy access" definition pandered by gun control advocates, it is still an illegal practice. Passing another law would not prevent this sort of occurrence. Enforcement of the existing law with full penalties for a conviction disqualifies the straw-buyer, but determined criminals will invariably find someone else to perform the same service.

The other primary target of scorn from gun prohibitionists is the so-called "gun show loophole." Under federal law, it has long been legal for private citizens to buy, sell or trade firearms without a federal license or without having to conduct a background check, so long as the individual is not "engaged in the business" of gun sales by conducting such sales on a volume basis.

For example, a person who attends a gun show can legally sell or trade some firearms from his personal collection on an occasional basis. However, if that individual repeatedly shows up at gun shows with dozens of guns to sell, and he/she purchases guns from others only to turn around and offer them for sale the same day or at the next gun show, it might be presumed that this individual is unlawfully dealing in firearms without a license.

A study conducted for the Department of Justice that involved interviews with thousands of convicted felons who had used guns in crimes determined that less than one percent had obtained their guns from gun shows. The overwhelming majority got their firearms through other means, and it is safe to conclude none of those transactions involved a direct purchase from a retail outlet, where a background check would have been conducted.

Some gun prohibitionists advocate requiring background checks for all gun transactions, but here, again, the notion that criminals will be tripped up by such a requirement is ludicrous. This is yet one more mechanism that inconveniences law-abiding citizens, among whom there are many who believe a more insidious purpose is behind the proposal. They are concerned that such a requirement would become a precursor for building a *de facto* gun registry.

And even if this were the case, gun rights advocates will quickly point out that it will not prevent a single violent crime.

Eight

YOU DON'T HUNT DUCKS WITH AN ASSAULT WEAPON

Q. *Why does anyone need a high-powered 'assault rifle?'*

Certainly one of the more successful Trojan Horse arguments in the on-going gun rights debate has been the question of "need."

Why does anyone "need" an "assault rifle" to hunt ducks or deer? Why does anyone "need" a semiautomatic handgun? Why does anyone "need" a handgun at all?

Here's a news flash for gun prohibitionists who will never agree that there is a legitimate need for any type of firearm: We have a Bill of *Rights* in this country, not a Bill of *Needs*. An American gun owner should not be obliged to demonstrate a "need" to own a firearm or a particular type of firearm, because that citizen has a fundamental civil right to own any kind of firearm he or she wants, the laws in California, Illinois, New Jersey, New York and elsewhere notwithstanding.

This right to own a firearm of one's choosing is simply intolerable for gun prohibitionists, who almost invariably deliver that "You don't *need...*" line with a sneer.

The late John Hosford, a retired Pierce County, WA sheriff's deputy who spent several years as executive director of the Citizens Committee for the Right to Keep and Bear Arms, once famously observed, "The day they say I can't have an 'assault rifle' is the day I am probably going to *need* one."

There have been some elitists in the firearms fraternity to actually subscribe to the "needs" argument, quite possibly for the sole purpose of offering some other kind of gun than they own; a sacrificial lamb on the altar of gun control, provided that nobody comes after *their* guns. This was most often demonstrated by skeet and trap shooters, who have never owned handguns, semiautomatic rifles or shotguns that had "no sporting purpose."

Such people are elitists in the true sense, for they see only *their* right to own the firearm of *their* choice, not the broader reality that other shooters and hunters have their own tastes.

That said, the elitist gun owners pale in comparison to the devoted gun prohibitionist in their disdain for firearms and the rights of gun owners. Indeed, they are loathe to even acknowledge – even in the wake of two affirmative Supreme Court rulings – that the Second Amendment actually affirms and protects a fundamental individual right to keep and bear arms, including handguns for self-defense. The Second Amendment is *not* about duck hunting. Many will insist that the high court was simply wrong.

The "needs" arguments that prohibitionists put forth are easy to refute.

Nobody needs a handgun to hunt deer.

This is a remarkably stupid argument, as many, if not a majority of states allow the hunting of deer and other big game with handguns. Several companies, including Sturm, Ruger, Smith & Wesson, Freedom Arms, Thompson/Center and Taurus have developed handguns in various calibers that are specifically designed for hunting.

Whether one "needs" a handgun for deer hunting is as ridiculous as challenging someone's "need" for a compound bow or a modern muzzleloading rifle, or a scope on his or her centerfire hunting rifle.

Big game handgun hunters do it for the challenge, the same as a bowhunter or a black powder hunter. Once this is established as the judging standard, then one finds that handgun hunters actually *need* the most powerful, flat-shooting and accurate handgun they can competently handle.

Handguns are designed only for killing people.

An equally preposterous contention, this belief has been handed down through generations of anti-gunners who have no working knowledge of competitive shooting and hunting, and they consider these endeavors to be repugnant.

Many handguns are specifically designed for hunting. A much broader family of handguns is designed for various levels of competition, from the traditional target models – either revolvers or semiautomatics – to the "race guns," which are pistols with design features that make them ideal for "action" shooting matches in which participants engage multiple targets where speed is an essential component.

These pistols and revolvers are not all the same, either in caliber or design. They range from the .22-caliber rimfire all the way up to .45-caliber, depending upon the particular sport.

Even the Olympics recognize shooting as a competitive sport, and there are so many local and regional competitions that it is impossible to track them all.

A significant segment of the competitive handgun community is devoted to metallic silhouette shooting, often at rather long ranges. The handguns designed for this game are highly stylized to the individual shooter, and they are anything but "typical" in a normal sense. They have adjustable sights, adjustable triggers, customized grips and other features that make them poor choices for offensive or defensive applications.

In recent years, "Cowboy Action" shooting has attracted thousands of participants, both men and women. They use old single-action revolvers, lever-action rifles and shotguns. Something of a cottage industry has erupted with clothing and other accoutrements to go along with the Cowboy theme of these events, and a significant segment of the firearms industry is devoted to replicating guns of that era for use by today's participants.

Nobody needs a semiautomatic assault rifle.

This is one of the greatest myths ever foisted on the public by the gun prohibition lobby. There is no such thing as a "semiautomatic assault rifle," unless one is discussing the WWII-era M1 Garand or its smaller sibling, the M1 carbine.

But, of course, these are not the rifles targeted by this clever misnomer. The modern "assault rifle," is a selective-fire weapon that can be fired either semi-auto (one shot per one squeeze of the trigger) or full-auto (several shots so long as the trigger is depressed).

Firearms demonized as assault rifles are look-alikes of military firearms and they function no differently than other types of semiautomatic rifles and shotguns. They only *look* different. Because of their typical black synthetic stocks and pistol grips, some consider them menacing in appearance.

However, the modern AR-type design has turned out to be the choice of a whole new generation of hunters and competitive shooters because they literally grew up with this type of firearm. Manufacturers including Remington, Rock River, Colt, Olympic Arms, DPMS and Sturm, Ruger have developed new calibers specifically for use in firearms built on the AR platform. These new rifles are ideally suited to hunting deer, antelope and other similar-sized game.

Even in their original 5.56mm NATO or .223 Remington chambering, these rifles have been adopted by legions of varmint and predator hunters, as well as competitive shooters. Firearms designers have developed heavier target-type barrels with faster rifling twists to improve accuracy in these rifles out to several hundred yards. Many of these guns are precision instruments and have no more use in combat than a rusty flintlock musket.

The modern bolt-action sporting rifle is an evolution from bolt-action military rifles from a century ago. They were, to use a phrase, the "assault rifle" of their era; a period during which armies still mounted bayonet charges from one muddy trench to another across fields criss-crossed by barbed-wire, and barren of anything else.

Indeed, certain semiautomatic AK/SKS variations chambered for the 7.62x39mm cartridge have become popular in many areas, where they are now called "the poor man's .30-30," a reference to the Model 94 Winchester or Model 336 Marlin lever-action rifles that were, for generations, *the* deer rifles in the big whitetail states from Maine to Minnesota. Ballistically, the cartridges are very similar. It's just that the guns chambered for the metric cartridge *look* different.

Nobody needs an "assault clip."

This is a more recent invention of the anti-gun lobby. The so-called "assault clip" is an extended-capacity pistol or rifle magazine that carries perhaps 15, 20 or more cartridges. Such magazines have various legitimate applications, including competition, recreational shooting, protection from coyotes, and home defense.

However, because Jared Lee Loughner and Seung Hui-Cho both used such magazines in their attacks, the Brady Campaign invented a new term to demonize these products. They have become "assault magazines." They argue that any magazine capable of holding more than ten cartridges is unnecessary. But what about magazines in guns carried by the police and soldiers?

That's different, of course, in the eyes of the gun prohibition lobby. They believe police and the military do not count when it comes to such limits. They might even argue that only police should have guns, a position this book addressed back in Chapter Three.

It is not simply the firepower that one of these magazines provides, though that is a critical point in the argument against then, but they also look menacing to the typical anti-gunner. And this brings them right back to their argument that nobody "needs" such an accessory, as though someone had appointed them as the arbiter of what people do and do not need.

J.R. Labbe, an editorial columnist with the *Fort Worth Star-Telegram* put this debate in its proper perspective following the attempted murder of Congresswoman Gabrielle Giffords. Labbe, the wife of a retired police officer, reacted to a drumbeat for renewal of the ban on so-called "assault weapons" and in particular high-capacity magazines, suddenly dubbed "assault clips." Labbe noted that talk about resurrecting the ban had set off a buying frenzy.

"The same folks who are buying the dickens out of them now were buying them in the 1990s when talk of that ban commenced," she wrote in early 2011. "They aren't criminals; they are sports enthusiasts and entrepreneurs. The fact that you don't have to wear body armor and take your kids to school behind a bulletproof shield proves that the preponderance of America's gun owners are responsible, law-abiding people with no interest in committing crime.

"The same question," she continued, "asked by supporters of the renewed ban was asked in 1994: Why does anyone need one of those? They should be left to the police and the military, not private citizens.

"Therein lies the main disconnect with gun-control advocates: They hold to the mistaken and potentially fatal belief that the police will be on hand to help them in their time of crisis," Labbe observed.

"Golly, they think, as long as I live in a community with a functioning 911 system, I don't need a firearm. And even if I do want a gun for personal protection, I've got Granddad's shotgun in the closet.

"Gun-rights advocates don't think that way," Labbe explained. "A self-reliant bunch as a whole, responsible gun owners don't want to leave it to a local deputy to make it to the house in time to stop the intruder who is jimmying the window to their kids' bedroom.

"As I have written before," she said, "it is not now and has never been the job of police to save your individual hide. A slew of court cases confirm that law enforcement is necessary to help keep societal peace, not to protect individual citizens."

Finally, Labbe concluded with a question that seems to sum it all up rather nicely.

"The question that gun-rights advocates want to respectfully pose to those adamant on restricting high-capacity magazine ownership is not 'Why does anybody need one?' but 'Why should responsible citizens not be allowed to own one'?"

Nobody needs to purchase more than one firearm a month.

How would this sound if someone were to suggest that "No woman needs to purchase more than one dress or one pair of shoes a month?" "No man needs more than one shirt."

Of course, the argument is specious, and you would create a furor among retailers at shopping malls all over.

The single significant difference in the gun versus dress or shirt argument is that nowhere in the Constitution is there any mention of shirts or dresses, but there is definitely mention of arms and the right to keep and bear them.

There is no credible evidence to suggest that one-gun-per-month rules have prevented a single crime from being committed anywhere in the United States. There may be some manufactured evidence, some manipulated evidence and considerable supposition based on the manufactured and manipulated evidence, but credibility is lacking.

Advocates of one-gun-per-month rules are convinced it will stop illegal gun trafficking. In actual practice, such rules have only made people who traffic in illegal guns a bit more clever in the strategies they use to get around such laws.

Let us look for a moment at the honest people such rules affect. Gun collectors would be in hopeless situations because they could neither buy nor sell more than one firearm in an effort to maintain their collections.

Hunters might be in trouble, in the event they buy a new gun prior to a hunt and find out they've gotten a lemon.

Competition shooters might also experience problems with such a statute, particularly someone new to the sport. Cowboy Action competitions require handguns, a rifle and a shotgun. Rarely does anyone see a Cowboy competitor with only one handgun, for example, and competitors in other shooting games frequently have more than one competition gun. We will return to this specific discussion in Chapter 12.

Why does anyone need to carry a hidden handgun?

Yet another favorite target of gun prohibitionists is a concealed carry law. The term "hidden handgun" is, itself, designed to elicit uneasiness in the general public, although the practice of openly carrying handguns has given anti-gunners fits in recent years. The gun prohibition lobby has feverishly testified against every concealed carry statute adopted over the past quarter-century, usually with the same stock arguments.

• Such laws will result in an escalation of violence.
• Such laws will cause more death among police officers and children.
• Such laws make it less safe for the general public.

The list of arguments goes on and on, yet there is no credible evidence that concealed carry statutes result in higher crime rates. There is some evidence that such laws may actually deter criminals, but in reality, adoption of concealed carry statutes does not necessarily change crime rates that much.

What is certain is that concealed carry laws *do not* result in higher crime rates and more violence. One prohibitionist group, the Violence Policy Center, has built a campaign against concealed carry laws by sensationalizing the comparatively small number of people whose licenses or permits are revoked because they are involved in some kind of crime, up to and including homicide. However, balanced against the more than 6 million citizens who are licensed to carry, this number is a tiny fraction.

People have a right to defend themselves and their families. This right is not limited to the confines of one's home. If criminally attacked in a place you have a right to be, you can defend yourself, and concealed carry enables the private citizen to have the tools to do that.

Nobody needs to keep a loaded gun in their home.

Millions of Americans keep firearms in their homes for personal protection and the protection of their families. Crime reports are filled with accounts of homeowners who successfully defend against burglary or home-invasion robbery, rape and other criminal assault, and even murder.

The famous 2008 Supreme Court ruling in *District of Columbia v. Dick Anthony Heller* was founded on the principle that people have a right to keep a gun in their home for personal protection, and that banning guns is unconstitutional. This was the case that set a precedent, defining the Second Amendment as protective of an individual civil right, and recognizing that handguns are commonly used for personal protection, and are thus protected by the Second Amendment.

Violent crime can happen so fast that the intended victims do not have the time nor the luxury of pausing events until they can retrieve a firearm from a gun safe or lock box, load it, and then defend themselves. In order for a firearm to be a useful piece of emergency survival equipment, it must be at the ready and it must be able to function properly. It would be the same as having to first unlock and then pump up a fire extinguisher before being able to put out that grease fire in the kitchen.

The philosophy that "nobody needs" this or that is put forth by people who consciously or subconsciously believe that society should exist by their individual standards.

It is like vegetarians preaching that nobody should eat meat. In the case of the gun prohibitionist, they tried to mandate their beliefs through passage of federal legislation. When that didn't work, they turned to the courts, but were ultimately not successful in that venue, either as the courts found time after time that firearms manufacturers cannot be held liable for the improper use of their functional products by third parties not under their control. Anti-gunners then returned to the legislative arena, at the state and local level, trying to accomplish in a patchwork fashion what they could not push through on a national scale. They also tried to commercially intimidate various companies, such as Starbucks, trying to have such companies ban the carrying of firearms on their premises.

This same exclusionary philosophy of the vegetarians exists among environmentalists who argue that nobody needs a pickup truck or SUV or other type of 4-wheel-drive vehicle, because they guzzle gasoline and leave a bigger carbon footprint, or maybe it is just because environmentalists don't drive such vehicles. (Never mind that some of the loudest proponents of green energy either drive SUVs or are chauffeured around in one).

Let us use as an example proponents of mass transit. They have quietly favored more expensive gasoline prices because they ultimately believe that higher prices at the pump will cause more people to rely on public transportation, thus leaving their cars and trucks parked at home.

In many parts of the American West, public transportation does not exist, and it is a long bicycle ride between highway rest stops. The answer: Move to a city, where one will naturally be encouraged to utilize public transportation.

Consider this for a moment: If government can mandate, or otherwise compel, masses of people to depend upon public transportation, then government can actually control your movement. Once government can control your movement, you are in trouble, and so are your neighbors, relatives and friends.

Likewise, if government can mandate that a person can only buy one gun per month, what is to prevent the same government from subsequently mandating only one gun purchase every six months, or one gun per year? We are not talking about stripping the Second Amendment from the Bill of Rights, because on paper, citizens would still have the right to keep and bear arms. However, by statute, that right becomes as limited and restrictive as possible without actually being abrogated.

This, ultimately, is precisely where the "needs" versus "rights" argument takes us, because on the "needs" level, the right to keep and bear arms becomes a heavily regulated privilege. This is already what anti-gun politicians in some states have accomplished, with such requirements as the Firearms Owners Identification Card in Illinois, or the lengthy permitting process in New York to even purchase a firearm, or requirements in New Jersey for owning and transporting handguns. All of these laws, and similar regulations in other jurisdictions were ostensibly adopted in an effort to fight crime and prevent human tragedy, but in reality, these statutes and ordinances have been increasingly utilized to discourage people from exercising their Second Amendment rights, or to punish them on some technical violation for having done so.

Keep this in perspective: Nobody has the right to tell the rest of us that we don't have any rights. It was this principle that convinced the Founding Fathers of the necessity to include the right to keep and bear arms in the Bill of Rights. They were concerned if not downright fearful of an oppressive government, and with that in mind, they affirmed through the Second Amendment that the people have the tools to resist, as a last resort. Today, of course, the liberal elite will dismiss that suggestion out of hand, possibly because the notion that a primitive guerilla-type force could never overcome the might of the U.S. military (presumably they think the entire military would be on the government's side in that kind of confrontation) and probably because the mere thought of resisting government is abhorrent to them.

One question to ask the liberals who think the U.S. military could never be successfully resisted is "What about the Viet Cong?" This hits a nerve with liberal elitists, many whom were anti-war protestors back in their college days of the 1960s and 1970s, and who were clearly sympathetic with the Viet Cong.

Where gun prohibitionists argue that "You don't need an assault rifle to hunt deer," the only proper response – and the one that is historically and legally accurate – is that The Second Amendment is *not about deer hunting*. It is, and always has been, about the right of the people to defend themselves and to resist tyranny. Liberals need to get over it.

On that subject, there is nothing in the Second Amendment about "sporting purposes." This invention was part of the Gun Control Act of 1968 dealing with the importation of certain types of firearms, and it fraudulent. Certain criteria were adopted in an effort to prevent some types of firearms from being imported, but an examination of historical documents relating to the Second Amendment and its background say nothing about "sporting purposes."

But let us, for a moment, return to the first premise of this chapter, the contention that "You don't need an assault weapon to hunt ducks." Again, the Second Amendment is *not* about duck hunting.

This remark ranks as being among the most inane and ill-informed in the English language because, if one analyzes the statement, it is utter nonsense, both historically and in practice.

People hunt ducks with shotguns, which are smoothbore weapons that are surprisingly adaptable to many uses. Anyone familiar with trench warfare in WWI, and with the use of shotguns during WWII and Southeast

Asia would recognize instantly that shotguns, with the proper configuration, are remarkably lethal assault weapons. The nickname "trench broom" did not just come from thin air. Shotguns were strategically used to "sweep" a trench of enemy combatants; that is, one or two rounds of buckshot fired from a shotgun could kill or severely wound several enemy soldiers at once.

Shotguns loaded with buckshot were devastating war instruments in the trenches of France in 1918. These shotguns were fitted with bayonet mounts, for engaging in hand-to-hand combat. In the Pacific during WWII, shotguns were used to shoot through jungle foliage, or to fire into a tunnel, makeshift bunker or cave. Ditto in the jungles of South Vietnam. Or they could be used to wreak havoc against multiple attacking enemy soldiers.

As far back as the Seven Years War (French and Indian War) in the 1750s, muskets loaded with buckshot were used against warring Indians, and smoothbore muskets loaded with buckshot found plenty of uses during the Revolutionary War, the Texas war of independence, Civil War, and upward through this country's history. These guns, thus loaded, were essentially the "assault shotguns" of their historical period, as were rifles of certain designs, as discussed earlier in this chapter.

Western lawmen and stagecoach guards "riding shotgun" (why do you think they called it that?) used the shotgun as an offensive and defensive weapon against road agents. On the other hand, the notorious California stagecoach bandit Black Bart, whose real name was Charles E. Boles, was often depicted as using a shotgun in his holdups.

Modern police carry shotguns in their patrol vehicles.

Do not be foolish enough to believe that shotguns have never been used as "assault weapons" because they have, and they will continue to be.

Military shotguns may *look* different than grandpa's prized Browning or Remington pump-action or autoloading shotgun that he takes out of the closet on weekends during the fall hunting season, but they function identically.

So, yes, you most certainly *do* use assault weapons for duck hunting. And for deer hunting, as is mandated in several states where the use of centerfire hunting rifles is prohibited. And for geese and wild turkeys during their respective hunting seasons. They may have longer barrels (though not always) and different sights, interchangeable chokes, maybe some fancy camouflage paint, but they are essentially the same guns used by today's military and police in terms of operation.

This revelation may be disturbing to some in the firearms fraternity who have tried to separate their particular favorite types of firearms from the kinds of guns that prohibitionists want to ban at any given moment, as we noted earlier in this chapter. Of course the failure of their logic is immediately clear to anyone who understands what a gun prohibitionist wants: Prohibition of privately owned firearms.

Today, it may be the AR-15. Tomorrow, the bolt-action hunting rifle with a telescopic sight that has suddenly become a "sniper rifle" just because they can be used to hit a target several hundred yards away. Next week, it may be the shotgun you use only at the skeet and trap range, targeted because it can fire the same ammunition as the WWI trench gun or the modern police shotgun.

So, the willingness of certain people to sacrifice someone else's favorite gun amounts to little more than a stopgap measure, and a rather selfish and short-sighted one at that.

Gun owners are all the same in the eyes of the prohibitionists, who may say today that you don't need an assault weapon to hunt ducks, and tomorrow tell you that you don't need a gun at all. That is because all guns are alike in the minds of the prohibitionists, who believe that firearms are meant for only one thing, to kill people, despite ample evidence to the contrary.

Perhaps the issue can be boiled down to something we have mentioned a few times in this chapter: the personal lifestyle of the prohibition advocate. That is, if the prohibitionist does not use something or like something, then he or she reasons that nobody should use or like that object or substance, either. It is the earmark of the extremist social engineer, to make everyone the same, in *their* image.

Nine

THE SECOND AMENDMENT IS OUTDATED

Q. *Isn't it about time to get over this notion that American citizens must have guns to defend their homes from outlaws and wild Indians, and repeal the Second Amendment?*

Ask any law enforcement officer about outlaws and so-called "wild Indians" from this nation's history and they might tell you that the marauders from bygone eras didn't hold a candle to today's crop of dangerous, violent criminals when it comes to mayhem and viciousness.

The question should be framed, *"Isn't it about time we get over this notion that citizens should surrender their right to be safe and secure from criminal attack just to make gun prohibitionist hoplophobes feel better?"* (A "hoplophobe" as defined by the late Col. Jeff Cooper, is someone who suffers from what he called "hoplophobia." That is, a "mental disturbance characterized by irrational aversion to weapons.")

The fact that the Bill of Rights was written more than 200 years ago does not really matter. One can argue all day long whether the Constitution is a "living document" but rest assured it is and always has been a *"legal* document" that still has all the relevance it enjoyed two centuries ago.

We still litigate cases over the First Amendment, and the Fourth and Fifth Amendments. The Brady Law's constitutionality was successfully challenged on Tenth Amendment grounds, not on Second Amendment grounds, and parts of that law were declared unconstitutional, a fact conveniently ignored by the mainstream press.

Yet this continuing debate over the relevancy of the Second Amendment leads one to ask some pertinent questions.

For example, do proponents of doing away with the Second Amendment think we can also get rid of the right against self-incrimination, and turn loose the rubber hose squad on criminal suspects until they confess to crimes they did not commit? Would they be comfortable with a system that compelled those accused of crimes to testify against themselves?

There really is a "slippery slope," and it starts with abandoning the Second Amendment, which for many people is the cornerstone of the Bill of Rights, and ultimately the Constitution as a whole. If we abolish the Second Amendment and erase it from the parchment, these citizens justifiably ask, what would be next?

Shall we give up the right to worship in the church or synagogue or mosque of our choice?

Do we forego search warrants and just allow police to invade our homes on legal fishing expeditions?

How about we empower the government to censor our news, or just do away with the news altogether because it is typically bad and very negative, and frequently critical of the government at one level or another?

Who needs bail or legal counsel to represent them in court? After all, if you weren't guilty, the police would never have arrested you in the first place!

It is one of the standing arguments of the anti-gun community; the contention that the Second Amendment long ago outlived its usefulness in the United States. The militia has been replaced by a powerful military and the National Guard. We have municipal police departments and county sheriffs, and more law enforcement agencies at the local, state and federal level than George Washington, Thomas Jefferson and James Madison ever dreamed could exist, perhaps even in their worst nightmares.

All of those men disliked the idea of a standing army. They viewed government service as a temporary duty, not a lifelong career; a philosophy that has sadly disappeared from the halls of Congress and state legislatures across the country.

With all of that, we still have a criminal element, and they are just as bold, probably more dangerous and certainly as bereft of moral character as their predecessors. Violent drug gangs would very possibly shock even the likes of Jesse James, Bob Dalton or John Wesley Hardin, all of whom committed various crimes and killed people. Hardin's individual record includes more than 30 killings.

Lest anyone forget, the Supreme Court ordered the State of California to release some 30,000 prisoners from confinement in mid-2011 because the Golden State simply did not have adequate space to house them all. Anyone who thinks that these people will return to their neighborhoods and turn their lives around, becoming productive citizens, is living in a fantasy world completely void of common sense.

Today's home invasion robberies are no less brutal than a war party attack on some frontier family's farm and cabin, and if you want to measure the difference in danger between some of today's neighborhoods with the OK Corral, the Earp-Clanton confrontation was minor league and self-contained. A shootout between warring drug gangs is far deadlier in terms of flying lead and its potential for collateral damage. Instead of an empty lot, such gun battles can encompass entire neighborhoods.

If the Second Amendment were outdated, one would hardly know it by the actions of Minneapolis, Minnesota resident Edward Curtis. The self-described "former" Marine, at age 61, managed to fight off a couple of men thought to be the infamous "Uptown Robbers" who were something of a single-entity crime wave in Minneapolis in early 2011.

According to published reports in the *Minneapolis Star Tribune*, Curtis was walking through a parking lot near his apartment one evening when the two suspects set upon him and began beating him. However, true to the principle that "once a Marine, always a Marine," Curtis fought back with his legally-carried pistol that the bad guys evidently did not see when they launched their nighttime attack.

Curtis reportedly got off three shots, and may have hit the two of the thugs before they beat a hasty retreat.

The Second Amendment could hardly be outdated because there is nothing outdated about self-defense and the ultimate human right of self-preservation. Advocates of gun prohibition have somehow lost sight of this important consideration. Their fear of firearms and the people who own them completely disregards the fundamental truth that defending one's self from grave bodily harm or death is made all the more difficult if one is denied the tools with which to accomplish the task.

The absurdity of gun prohibition was perhaps best illustrated in an opinion piece written by Philadelphia-based freelance writer Lee Gaillard, which appeared in the *Seattle Times* in early 2008, the period leading up to the landmark Supreme Court Second Amendment ruling in *District of Columbia v. Dick Anthony Heller*. Gaillard subscribes to the thoroughly refuted "collectivist theory" regarding the Amendment. He considered it applicable only to some right of the states to organize and maintain a militia.

Gaillard, like so many other individual rights opponents, focused his attention on the first clause of the Amendment: "A well regulated Militia being necessary to the security of a free State..." Prior to the *Heller* ruling, and for a while after it, anti-gunners vigorously insisted that there is not, and never has been, an individual civil right to keep and bear arms, and that Associate Justice Antonin Scalia had deliberately re-written history to suit his conservative agenda.

"Given the Founders' original intent clearly contained in that introductory absolute phrase," Gaillard wrote, "the consequently irrelevant Second Amendment should be long gone…"

His contention was thoroughly demolished in the majority opinion in the *Heller* case, authored by Justice Scalia. Here is what Scalia actually said about the collectivist/militia theory, demonstrating that he put some careful and exhaustive research into his words:

> *It is therefore entirely sensible that the Second Amendment's prefatory clause announces the purpose for which the right was codified: to prevent elimination of the militia.*
>
> *The prefatory clause does not suggest that preserving the militia was the only reason Americans valued the ancient right; most undoubtedly thought it even more important for self-defense and hunting. But the threat that the new Federal Government would destroy the citizens' militia by taking away their arms was the reason that right—unlike some other English rights—was codified in a written Constitution. Justice Breyer's assertion that individual self-defense is merely a 'subsidiary interest' of the right to keep and bear arms…is profoundly mistaken. He bases that assertion solely upon the prologue – but that can only show that self-defense had little to do with the right's codification; it was the central component of the right itself.*

It is not until later in his Op-Ed piece that Gaillard exposes the true mindset of the gun prohibitionist, however:

> *We obviously have access to firearms. People facing potentially dangerous workplace confrontations can apply for concealed-weapon permits; buying a rifle to hunt deer poses no problem.*
>
> *On the other hand, there's a huge difference between sporting rifles and high-cyclic-rate-of-*

fire weapons designed to suppress enemy defenses during military assaults — in the process disabling or killing as many human beings as possible. Despite Congress' failure to renew the assault-weapons ban, there is no justification for civilians to possess machine pistols or semiautomatic rifles.

With our nation already awash in more than a quarter of a billion firearms — deadly weapons all — the government must enforce measures ensuring that criminal-background checks are performed on all purchasers, that such weapons are registered, the owners licensed, and all losses and thefts reported...

Lives are already being lost as the deadly deluge of firearms inundates Detroit, Philadelphia and other besieged cities — overwhelming police departments and slaughtering citizens: In 2005, 846 American service members died in Iraq while 10,100 U.S. civilians died from gunshot wounds.

The Second Amendment disappears atop the frothing surge of hundreds of millions of already 'owned' guns flooding our streets. The Supreme Court needs to dismiss District of Columbia v. Heller as inapplicable, handing down instead a decision concerning the level at which these deadly weapons are to be regulated for public safety.

This is the kind of hysteria-laden extremist rhetoric that all-too-typically forms the cornerstone of the gun prohibition argument. It is emotional, gut-level boilerplate, and that's all it is. A careful reading of Justice Scalia's *Heller* opinion should remove any doubt that the Framers intended the Second Amendment to affirm the right of individual citizens to keep and bear arms.

In early 2011, the Citizens Committee for the Right to Keep and Bear Arms and the Second Amendment Foundation launched a mobile billboard campaign that visited several cities. The message it carried was brief and blunt:

2,191 Americans uses guns in self-defense every day.
Guns Save Lives.

The figure was based on the total estimate of armed self-defense actions over the course of a year, divided by 365. Between 800,000 and 2.5 million firearm uses are estimated to prevent criminal actions annually. The campaign drew good crowds everywhere it appeared, whether in Los Angeles, Chicago, Washington, D.C., Phoenix, Milwaukee, Las Vegas, Pittsburgh (during the 2011 convention of the National Rifle Association), Miami and several other cities, occasionally in deliberate conflict with or immediately following some type of gun control effort.

Does that make it seem as though the Second Amendment should be repealed? To the chagrin of people like Gaillard and the anti-gun Brady Campaign, and the Violence Policy Center and others in the gun prohibition movement, whenever the public speaks on the Second Amendment, the majority embraces the individual right concept. Whenever gun control measures are placed on the ballot, they invariably fail. The proposed California handgun ban failed miserably. The Massachusetts anti-gun measure failed. An initiative calling for licensing and registration in Washington State was crushed.

It is this consistent public sentiment that leaves the gun prohibition lobby "shooting blanks" when they advocate for gun bans or gun laws that are so restrictive that they essentially constitute a gun ban. Once the public is able to clearly understand the details of various gun control proposals, citizens consistently reject them.

So, why do gun control advocates continue to push their disarmament agenda?

It is easy to argue that the liberal anti-gun mindset simply abhors firearms, and sees them perhaps only as a necessary evil when carried and wielded by police or the military.

Of course, the problem reaches much deeper than that. Earlier in this chapter, we used a term: "hoplophobe."

This is a person who suffers from a psychological affliction defined by the late Col. Jeff Cooper, a world-renowned firearms advocate and instructor, philosopher and Marine Corps veteran, that is now part of the American lexicon.

Hoplophobia, as Cooper explained it, derives from the Greek word *hoplon*, which translates to armor. Hoplophobia is further defined as a fear of firearms and/or armed citizens. It is described as such by Wikipedia.

Cooper is credited with actually inventing the term, using it to label what he considered an "irrational aversion to weapons" and particularly firearms. Many anti-gun people are simply frightened at the sight of a firearm. The authors have seen this aversion many times. They are particularly fearful of firearms in the hands of private citizens, quite possibly because they subconsciously transfer their own inexperience with firearms to others who have guns, and thus fear that the gun owner is no more familiar with firearms than they are themselves. The inevitable result of this, the hoplophobe fears, will be a deadly firearms accident.

On one occasion at the Washington State capitol in Olympia in early 2010, the state's leading anti-gunner appeared to testify in support of a proposed ban on so-called "assault rifles." Also in attendance were about 200 gun rights activists, among whom were approximately two dozen Open Carry advocates. They were visibly armed, which is perfectly legal on the capitol campus.

The gun control advocate was observed talking frantically to a State Patrol trooper assigned to the capitol security detail. The advocate demanded to know why these people were allowed to be armed, and them demanded to know whether state troopers had checked each gun to see whether it was loaded (they all were!). The lieutenant in charge of the detail that day patiently told this fellow that there was no law against it, and that his troopers had no statutory authority to check the condition of each firearm.

The hearing transpired without incident, and the gun control lobbyist quickly departed, leaving several armed gun rights activists to chat at their leisure with reporters.

Some gun prohibitionists fear firearms because of some personal tragedy, such as the accidental death or deliberate slaying of a loved one. Others are simply afraid of being hurt, and so they advocate being a submissive victim when confronted with a criminal act. Rarely does one encounter a true pacifist; someone who absolutely refuses to use force or advocate the use of force, even at the risk of their own safety.

More typically, gun prohibitionists are all too happy to see force used in their defense, i.e. the killing of Osama bin Laden by Navy SEALS or the use of force by armed police to interrupt a crime. It does not occur to the gun prohibitionist that police and members of the armed forces are citizens like themselves, except that police and soldiers understand that sometimes force, even lethal force, is necessary for the common good.

Such people are advocates of the "collective right" theory about the Second Amendment; that it applies only to arming the military and, in a tortured logic, arming the police, but not private citizens. They are comfortable with "authority figures" being armed, but they vehemently dislike the idea of private citizens being armed because that enables the armed private citizen to act with some authority in the defense of himself and others.

Some have argued that this suggests a psychological aversion to individualism; that is, people who would subscribe to the "collectivist" Second Amendment theory more deeply associate themselves with an overall "collective" mindset and lifestyle. They find it alarming that citizens just like them may have an independent streak. Such individuals don't need to "call a repairman" because they can fix things, themselves, whether it involves changing a flat tire or the oil in one's car, or working on the wiring in one's own home, or defending one's self and one's family from imminent and unavoidable harm or death, when it seems much more acceptable to dial 9-1-1 and wait for the police to respond.

Ultimately, it translates to the realization that individualists can take care of themselves, and do not need shepherds. This is why one frequently finds members of the firearms community referring to such people as "sheep" who believe they are protected by shepherds and sheep dogs (government and police). Gun owners, on the other hand, do not see themselves as members of a flock to be preyed upon.

Resentment among gun prohibitionists toward the Second Amendment and people who exercise their right to keep and bear arms is almost boundless. Following the Supreme Court's historic 2008 *Heller* ruling that affirmed the Second Amendment protects an individual civil right, some anti-gunners wanted to repeal the amendment. The high court did not rule in their favor, so their response is to be rid of the offensive Second Amendment. Childish as that seemed at the time, many anti-gun-rights advocates were convinced this was the proper avenue to take, and they remain adamant about it today.

Arguing for repeal was, evidently, a far better option than simply accepting the court ruling and living with it, as gun prohibitionists would argue that gun owners learn to "live with" the loss of their firearms freedoms.

This takes us back a few paragraphs to the point about sheep. For the ardent gun hater, accepting the fact that gun ownership is a protected civil right has never been an acceptable option. Comparable, perhaps, to the behavior of a spoiled child, the gun prohibitionist wants it his or her way, period, as if the world revolved around their personal morals and mores.

In the final analysis, this is perhaps why facts do not matter, and never will, to people whose goal is the abolition of private firearms ownership. Nothing less is acceptable. Yes, there is evidence that firearms are used by bad people to do bad things to good people or other bad people. Yes there is data to show people are injured or killed in firearms mishaps. But there is also abundant information about lives saved and criminal acts deterred thanks to the presence of a firearm.

Instead of taking a rational approach to the problem; i.e. learning from mishaps and crime patterns and taking corrective measures, the prohibitionist has settled instead to push for a total elimination of a civil right. No important facts about the benefits of gun ownership, no data on the decline in firearms accidents and fatalities over the past half-century; none of it would sway the ardent anti-gunner toward re-evaluation of his or her position. They refuse to accept any possibility that their position is wrong.

Tell the gun prohibitionist that hunter education classes taught to a couple of generations of American youngsters have contributed to an overall reduction in hunting and firearm-related accidents, and they may offer lip service to the program but are not impressed by the results. Explain how armed citizens have prevented or intervened in violent confrontations, perhaps saving lives in the process, and anti-gunners will insist this is an aberration and that such instances are rare. They simply dismiss the evidence because it conflicts with their agenda.

What will be offered in rebuttal are chronicles of school shootings, brutal armed robberies, anecdotal stories about this or that young crime victim?

They will argue that the NRA or CCRKBA or other gun rights groups never compromise. Compromise in their lexicon translates to gun rights organizations accepting whatever terms gun prohibitionists wish to offer, without negotiation and without offering anything in return. All the while, one might add, the firearms groups have the Constitution and Supreme Court rulings on their side.

As noted earlier, the Constitution may or may not be a so-called "living document" that can be amended, but it most definitely is a legal document that spells out certain individual rights and places limits on government. The Bill of Rights does not "grant" anything, nor does it "create" rights out of thin air. It recognizes that the rights it protects – those rights delineated in its ten amendments – were individual human rights. The Constitution and Bill of Rights merely affirms and protects these rights.

Gun prohibitionists are big on certain rights, but seem to share a common philosophy that they can pick and choose from a smorgasbord of civil rights, recognizing and honoring some and ignoring others. The Bill of Rights does not work that way and was never designed to work that way. The Founders understood that these rights exist whether they are put on paper or not, a philosophy that appears to have escaped gun control advocates over the years. Gun banners appear to erroneously believe that if they simply repeal the Second Amendment, removing its text from the Bill of Rights, the right to keep and bear arms will simply disappear.

Subsequently, many gun prohibitionists believe that laws will then be adopted that force people to turn in their firearms, or allow them to be seized. Such thinking is delusional at best, even though British subjects and citizens of Australia turned in lots of guns following the adoption of restrictive legislation in those countries.

The United States is different terrain, politically and philosophically. A national gun turn-in on the scale that would satisfy the gun prohibition lobby will never happen because the people simply would not stand for it, nor would they willingly cooperate with it.

This was made especially clear after the Supreme Court ruling against the State of California, which forced the release of thousands of prison inmates due to overcrowding. Timing could not have been worse because with budget crises facing various local governments and the state, police agencies simply did not have the manpower to deal with that kind of situation, and police administrators acknowledged that.

One critic of the high court's ruling even alluded to arming one's self.

"What is the message for law-abiding people in California," asked Kent Scheidegger with the Criminal Justice Legal Foundation, based in Sacramento on his Internet blog. "Buy a gun. Get a dog. Put in an alarm system. Even seriously consider bars on the windows."

Obviously Scheidegger recognized that there are ample reasons for gun ownership today, and without the Second Amendment, that option would not be available for consideration.

Even where people seem to embrace restrictive gun laws, when an alarming situation develops that could directly affect them in a very unpleasant way, they will almost reflexively reach for a gun, or at least the opportunity to own one. Face it, there is something comforting about having a firearm when one's personal safety is being threatened. Recall the surge in gun purchasing following the Sept. 11, 2001 terrorist attacks. That event was the catalyst for many first-time firearm purchases by people who had never before considered owning a gun. Some prominent Washington, D.C. insiders are known to have very quietly taken self-defense shooting lessons in the wake of that attack.

The late actor Charlton Heston once related how, during the 1992 Rodney King Riots, several of his Hollywood acquaintances – apparently all anti-gunners – contacted him for the loan of a firearm, evidently in the belief that he had plenty of guns to spare. Heston's gun ownership and his leanings toward the Second Amendment were widely known in Tinsel Town, so he recalled the irony of the situation when people who had supported all sorts of gun control measures asked him for a firearm when their own safety was in jeopardy.

Images of shop owners firing at rioters from the rooftops of their businesses are stark reminders of the importance, not only of strong self-defense tradition among the citizens in this country, but also having the necessary tools to defend themselves.

Hypocrisy seems to abound among gun prohibitionists. Those who can afford it often have personal bodyguards, and others live in gated communities or large apartment buildings. Still others have firearms that they simply will not acknowledge, as this would reveal them as the hypocrites they are.

A fundamental civil right never becomes outdated. Ask those who fought for right-to-carry laws in dozens of states. Ask the border-area residents of Arizona, New Mexico and Texas about the importance of the Second Amendment to their personal safety in an era when drug runners and human traffickers habitually cross private lands as they bring their illegal cargos north from Mexico. Ask any crime victim who has successfully defended himself or herself from violent criminal attack, or the attack of a vicious animal.

Making the personal choice to *not* exercise the right to keep and bear arms under the Second Amendment is no reason to demand that everyone else be forced to make the same adjustment to their individual liberty by abolishing the right. This is not advocated in the noble interest of equality, but in the selfish interest of conformity.

Perhaps it could be said that the one thing hoplophobes are truly phobic about is not firearms *per se*, but the fact that gun owners can fend for themselves and be self-sufficient. Individualism seems to offend and alarm such people, and those emotions are amplified when the individual has the tools with which to exert that individuality, and defend it.

Ten

GUN PERMITS SHOULD BE PUBLIC RECORD

Q. *Why shouldn't newspapers have access to the names and addresses of citizens who are licensed to carry? Isn't such disclosure in the best interest of public safety?*

Frankly, there is no good reason for newspapers to acquire and then publish the identity of any law-abiding private citizen who exercises his or her right to keep and bear arms, but there are plenty of bad ones.

The claim by newspapers that such disclosure is in the interest of public safety is a canard and they know it. Author Workman has been in journalism for four decades, and in his opinion, publishing those names, or even demanding access to that information, is an invasion of privacy and borders on journalistic voyeurism.

Newspapers are in the business of selling news, and nothing sells like sensationalism. Printing the names of armed *private* citizens causes a sensation, especially among people who dislike guns and those who own them.

The "inconvenient truth" about most news rooms and editorial boards is that they are almost wholly populated by people with liberal political leanings. Though they may be the last to acknowledge this and would do so only reluctantly because it justifiably could expose them to accusations of bias, reporters and editors with but the rare exception are more likely to support gun control measures than oppose them, same as they are more likely to vote for Democrats than Republicans.

A textbook example of this bias surfaced during the debate in Wisconsin over adoption of a concealed carry statute. Wisconsin, until 2011, had never allowed concealed carry despite adoption of such laws in 48 other states. Former Gov. Jim Doyle, an anti-gun Democrat, twice vetoed legislation before he was replaced by Republican Scott Walker.

Though perhaps not representative of every newsroom in the country, comments by *Milwaukee Journal Sentinel* columnist Eugene Kane put into perspective how far too many members of the Fourth Estate view gun rights.

"Actually," Kane wrote, "Republicans are considering two versions of the concealed carry law, which I would label thusly: There's the 'sane' bill and the 'insane' bill.

"The sane version - which I oppose - would allow gun owners to apply for permits and receive required training to carry concealed weapons in most public areas but with some restrictions. The insane version - which I vehemently oppose - would allow gun owners to carry concealed weapons in public without any permit or training required."

Translation: Kane is content using his First Amendment right to stand in the way of Wisconsin citizens exercising their Second Amendment right. He would not be agreeable to any kind of carry measure, period.

By publishing the identities of concealed carry permit holders, the newspaper deliberately and some might suggest maliciously exposes these people to possible public scorn and ridicule, though a newspaper editor or reporter would never acknowledge that as their motive. They invariably argue that such a probe is for the public good, and that the public has a right to know who among them may be carrying a firearm.

The public has no such right.

The average gun owner is not a public official nor a public figure, so there is no compelling public interest in revealing whether John Smith or Jane Jones has a permit to carry a firearm for their personal protection. Indeed, for their own safety, it might be far better to withhold such information about Mr. Smith or Ms. Jones from public dissemination.

Newspaper fascination with such information is part of a much broader attack on the exercise of Second Amendment rights, and it smacks of using sensationalism to sell newspapers; an act of crass hypocrisy because, while the newspaper bemoans the fact that citizens are armed, they figure out a way to make a profit by exposing their identities. For some years, a campaign has been waged by gun prohibitionists that encourages parents to ask whether some other family has guns in the home. This effort is pandered as being in the interest of safety for children, but there is a subliminal reason for making such inquiries.

It sets up gun owning families, and particularly their children, for social ostracism. Gun prohibitionists know this, evidently having concluded that if they cannot browbeat people into giving up their guns, they will embarrass them into doing it through social pressure on their children.

Not far removed from this effort are family practitioners who, as part of their patient questionnaires, ask whether a family has firearms in the home. Some doctors and medical clinics, upon learning that there are guns in a home, presume to offer gun safety advice.

Unless a physician or a nurse is a certified firearms instructor, they have no business engaging in such a boundary violation. In 2011, Florida passed legislation penalizing physicians for making such inquiries. It set off a political firestorm as anti-gunners protested and filed a lawsuit to overturn the law.

For whatever reason beyond mere commercial exploitation, there has been something of an animosity in this nation's newsrooms toward the Second Amendment.

This is hardly a new phenomenon. It has been going on for years.

The late Thomas Winship, former editor of the *Boston Globe* and a columnist in *Editor & Publisher*, wrote in the latter for its April 24, 1993 edition that newspapers should "Investigate the NRA with renewed vigor. Print names of those who take NRA funds. Support all causes the NRA opposes. ... The work a day guy doesn't envision total confiscation, but many with the real power to sway public opinion and effect change in America do."

Urging in his column to "step up the war against guns," Winship encouraged his colleagues at copy desks across the country to "place all youth killings on Page One, as the *Chicago Tribune* does." He wanted editors to target gun manufacturers, and to argue for strict licensing. Winship was hardly alone in his dislike for firearms.

Michael Gartner, then president of NBC News, wrote in *USA Today* that "There is no reason for anyone in this country, anyone except a police officer or a military person, to buy, to own, to have, to use a handgun.

"I used to think handguns could be controlled by laws about registration, by laws requiring waiting periods for purchasers, by laws making sellers check out the past of buyers.

"I now think the only way to control handgun use in this country is to prohibit the guns. And the only way to do that is to change the Constitution."

TIME Magazine's Roger Rosenblatt argued for getting "rid of the damned things" in a column about guns when he wrote, "My guess [is] . . . that the great majority of Americans are saying they favor gun control when they really mean gun banishment. . . . I think the country has long been ready to restrict the use of guns, except for hunting rifles and shotguns, and now I think we're prepared to get rid of the damned things entirely – the handguns, the semis and the automatics."

That quote and the next one were dredged up by L. Brent Bozell in a column he did for the *Washington Times*. Bozell quoted *TIME* national correspondent

Jack E. White, who wrote, "Whatever is being proposed is way too namby-pamby. I mean, for example, we're talking about limiting people to one gun purchase or handgun purchase a month. Why not just ban the ownership of handguns when nobody needs one? Why not just ban semi-automatic rifles? Nobody needs one."

Nobody has suggested that these individuals, and many others in journalism who are just like them, do not have a right to hold personal opinions about firearms ownership. However, no member of the press has the right to allow his personal politics color his approach to the news. And, it could be said, after people like Rosenblatt "guess" that the majority of Americans want "gun banishment," that these journalists are at the very least arrogant, and quite possibly delusional. The role of the press is to be a watchdog on government, to report news accurately and fairly. Advocacy should be left to the editorial page, not turned into activism in the news columns, and the editorial activism should be based on some credible data or premise, not merely the "guess" that what you advocate is what the "great majority of Americans are saying."

For newspapers to publicly identify gun owners who are licensed to carry could easily be considered as a form of harassment. Newspaper editors justify this badgering with the rhetoric of lofty ideals about public safety. It is a façade, a flimsy sham that masks their true motive, which is to perpetuate a rather personalized campaign against the Second Amendment.

All of this can be boiled down to a single definition: Journalistic demagoguery.

During the debate about concealed carry legislation in Wisconsin in the spring of 2011 – the Badger State had never had a concealed carry law and, as noted earlier, previous attempts to pass one were vetoed by former Gov. Doyle – both the *Milwaukee Journal Sentinel* and *Green Bay Gazette* advocated making the names of permit recipients public. Both newspapers couched their remarks in terms of promoting open government, but beyond that offered no clear reason for wanting the information.

Such information might be useful to residential burglars, who could easily track down the addresses of people who have concealed carry permits, then break in when the homeowners are away at work, figuring that they would find a firearm or several guns.

How about abusive former spouses or domestic partners? Would it be to their advantage to know whether their "ex" might have gotten a carry permit?

Ultimately, it is nobody's business if someone owns a firearm. So long as the armed citizen is responsible with his or her gun, doesn't violate any law or hurt anyone, why should anyone care if they have a carry permit?

When a newspaper engages in this kind of public exposure effort, it is attempting to bully gun owners who have committed no crime. There is no justifiable reason to place any of these citizens in the public spotlight for merely exercising a civil right and otherwise going about their daily routines. Unjustifiably stigmatizing private citizens does not fall within the normal routine of a newspaper.

On the other hand, it would be useful for newspapers to ask pertinent questions about gun permits when investigating shootings. Why there is a reluctance to do this makes less sense than publishing the names of law-abiding gun owners, because in the case of a criminal investigation, there *is* a compelling reason for the public to know the identity of the shooter, especially if he is being sought by the authorities, and may be at large, armed and potentially dangerous.

Perhaps newspaper reporters don't ask whether the suspect in a criminal shooting investigation had a concealed pistol license or permit because they know that in the overwhelming majority of such cases, the gunman does not have such a permit. Indeed, in many of these cases, the perpetrator is either too young to be carrying a handgun because they are underage for a permit, or they are altogether disqualified from possessing a gun because of prior criminal convictions.

Gun prohibitionists and anti-gun reporters and commentators are loathe to make the distinction because it would telegraph to the readers that the crime, whatever it happened to be, was *not* the work of a legally-licensed armed citizen, but of some lowlife. It is precisely the activities of such outlaws that compel many people to obtain carry permits in the first place because like it or not, there are typically only two people at the scene of a crime in progress, the perpetrator and the victim(s). Police are minutes away, at the very least, and sometimes hours away.

To reveal the names of legally-licensed private citizens to the entire community is a modern approach to placing upon them a Scarlet letter, or perhaps a Star of David. Ultimately the same mentality appears to be at work.

Like it or not, in today's newsrooms, social bigotry against gun owners and the Second Amendment is still acceptable. Why managing editors or newspaper ombudsmen rarely question this hostility might be a mystery to some, but it may be that these managers and internal watchdogs don't detect the hostility because they share the same opinions. This anti-gun bigotry can be practiced in various ways, and publicly identifying gun owners, or merely threatening to do that as a means of harassment and intimidation, is just one form.

Why do they do it? Because they can get away with it.

The manner in which a self-defense shooting is reported is another way, and the complete omission of certain facts is yet another. Reporters can deliberately misinform their readers about firearms. One such example is the term "high-powered assault rifle," a term that is both inflammatory and technically inaccurate.

Reporters and copy editors can mislabel firearms as "automatic weapons" when they are in actuality semi-automatic by design.

Some in the press have adopted a new term invented by the anti-gun Brady Campaign, the "assault clip," a reference to the cartridge magazine of a rifle or pistol that holds more than ten rounds. It matters not to these people that firearms were designed with such magazines, nor do the reporters care that millions of private citizens own such magazines and the firearms that go with them, while having never harmed a soul.

There is some credibility to the argument put forth by gun-owning press critics that it is because of this penchant among newspaper reporters to quickly adapt the buzz words of gun prohibitionists that firearms owners have cancelled their newspaper subscriptions. That certainly would not bring a business to its knees, but losing an entire readership bloc cannot be healthy for a newspaper's survival because declines in readership typically mean the newspaper cannot charge as much for its advertising, and that definitely affects the bottom line.

The same can be said about sportsmen, and especially hunters. Newspapers that reduce or eliminate their outdoors sections, or shift the emphasis from consumptive sports to things like rock climbing, bird watching and cross-country skiing consciously abandon a readership that, 50 years ago, was remarkably strong. Many hunters subscribed to newspapers simply to read the outdoors sections. That is no longer the case.

It is the deliberate rejection of pro-gun, or at least neutral firearms news and hunting-related coverage that reinforces the notion that newspapers not only do not care about that reader bloc, they are overtly hostile toward them. Thus, a newspaper has no qualms about launching a campaign to "out" gun owners to their neighbors in the interest of sensationalism. They are not worried about losing those readers, because they already surrendered them and cut them adrift.

As this book was being written, Washington State revealed that more than 337,000 citizens had active concealed pistol licenses. If you were an Evergreen State resident, would you want your name and other information revealed on the pages of the *Seattle Times* or the *Spokane Spokesman-Review*? Fortunately the names of CPL holders are confidential. Anti-gunners may not like this because the law leaves them without what many consider an important tool – intimidation through harassment – in their battle to eliminate firearms rights.

But what if Washington did not have such protection for its legally-armed private citizens? Can anyone imagine the state's leading newspapers would not go after that information? What would the *Everett Herald* do with access to the names of 337,000 citizens who are licensed to carry? They could name every individual residing in Snohomish County, where Everett is located, and who has a CPL. The *Seattle Times* would almost certainly demand a list of every CPL holder in King County

It is an interesting strategy that other newspapers have used to simply annoy gun owners in their readership area. As noted a few paragraphs earlier, newsrooms have, at least in some cases, taken on the appearance of being openly hostile towards gun owners and hunters. The urge to publish information about concealed carry permit holders is one of the higher-profile examples of that hostility.

What should be noted repeatedly is that revealing the names and addresses of gun owners and concealed pistol permit holders has never been shown to have prevented a single crime. Lacking any data to show a crime decline after such information is published should be proof enough for any reasonable person that this information does not need to be publicized. Neighborhoods are no more or less safe than they would be if the information remains confidential.

Eleven

REPORTING AND REGISTERING SALES KEEPS GUN DEALERS HONEST

Q. *Why shouldn't we monitor, report and register sales of all firearms if it means we can stop illegal gun trafficking?*

Remember this name: "Operation Fast and Furious." We discussed it in some detail in Chapter Five, and now we are going to probe deeper into the government "sting" operation that was so deplorable in its nature, and in administration attempts to cover it up and shift blame when it went bad, that it may one day be remembered as a scandal worse than Watergate, which unfolded almost 40 years earlier and forced – for the first time in history – the resignation of the President of the United States, Richard Nixon.

That is, of course, if media cheerleaders for the Obama administration forget their politics and fulfill their professional responsibility to present the facts and allow the American public to make up its own mind. It will probably be left to historians to determine just how bad the scandal was. One thing is certain, and that is the difference between Watergate and Fast-and-Furious: Nobody was killed because of Watergate.

Six months to the day after the slaying of Border Patrol agent Brian Terry in the desert of southern Arizona, the House Committee on Oversight and Government Reform convened a blockbuster hearing on Operation Fast and Furious, the controversial would-be gunrunning sting mounted by the Bureau of Alcohol, Tobacco, Firearms and Explosives' field office in Phoenix. It was this botched operation that, by some estimates, put as many as 2,500 guns into the hands of Mexican drug cartels, while ATF officials in Phoenix and Washington, D.C. encouraged the program even after repeated protests and concerns were voiced by field agents and retail firearms dealers.

Before the gavel fell on that four-hour hearing, chaired by Congressman Darrell Issa (R-CA), reporters in the room and viewers watching it on C-Span or YouTube would be stunned and shocked. They would hear from three whistleblower ATF agents who repeatedly discussed, under oath, about being ordered to allow guns to be "walked" out of retail stores and into the hands of suspected gun smugglers. They would hear from the family of slain agent Terry. They would hear from U.S. Senator Charles Grassley, who related his months of frustration at being stonewalled by the ATF and Justice Department in his attempts to probe the Fast and Furious operation.

And, they would hear from an assistant attorney general who seemed more adept at *not* answering questions than he was at providing direct responses.

In the process, America learned that the ATF acting director had been able to monitor suspected straw sales of guns to gunrunning suspects from his office nearly 2,000 miles away, thanks to hidden cameras and direct video links. In testimony given in secret, then Acting Director Kenneth Melson denied having actually watched such a sale in progress. They learned that gun dealers and field agents had warned against the strategy, predicting – accurately as it turned out – that letting these guns get into the hands of criminals would result in countless innocent deaths, and possibly (most assuredly) the death of a law enforcement officer.

Perhaps not surprisingly to anyone familiar with politics, Melson would ultimately become one of the key witnesses for the Issa committee and the Fast-and-Furious investigation. He met with congressional investigators, accompanied by his own attorney, secretly on July 4, 2011 to prevent Justice Department officials from learning about the appearance and intervening. It was during that meeting, in which he provided sworn testimony, that he began to unravel what was now appearing like a cover-up attempt at the highest levels of the Justice Department.

"My view is that the whole matter of the Department's response in this case was a disaster," Melson told investigators, according to a transcript of the interview. "That as a result, it came to fruition that the (House) committee staff had to be more aggressive and assertive in attempting to get information from the Department, and as a result, there was more adverse publicity towards ATF than was warranted if we had cooperated from the very beginning. And a lot of what they did was damage control after a while. Their position on things changed weekly and it was hard for us to catch up on it, but it was very clear that they were running the show."

Perhaps even more damaging to the Obama administration and the Justice Department under Attorney General Eric Holder was Melson's assertion that the department was trying to shift blame away from political appointees.

"It was very frustrating to all of us," Melson told investigators, "and it appears thoroughly to us that the department is really trying to figure out a way to push the information away from their political appointees at the department."

Most important of all, investigators would learn that while the Obama administration started pointing fingers of blame in 2009 at American firearms dealers for the violence in neighboring Mexico, the real culprits for putting so many guns into illegal circulation may have been the officials at

ATF and the Justice Department who originally devised this scheme and then encouraged dealers to cooperate, and individuals who were possibly paid informants for the Federal Bureau of Investigation.

Topping it all off, the entire operation was founded on what several journalists, including columnist Jack Kelly with the *Pittsburgh Post-Gazette*, revealed as something of a fraud. We discussed this in an earlier chapter. Here's what Kelly had to say about Obama administration claims that 90 percent of guns recovered at Mexican crime scenes came from the United States:

> *More than 90 percent of the guns recovered in Mexico come from the United States, many from gun shops that line our border," President Barack Obama said in 2009.*
>
> *That isn't true. Of 100,000 guns recovered by Mexican authorities, only 18,000 came from the United States, ATF Deputy Assistant Director Bill McMahon testified. Of these, just 7,900 came from sales by licensed gun dealers.*
>
> *Though Mr. Obama's false claim was debunked right away -- nearly 90 percent of the traceable guns Mexican authorities turned over to U.S. officials came from the United States, not 90 percent of the guns they confiscated -- administration officials kept making it. Could "Fast and Furious" have been an effort to make it appear to be true?*

Documents presented during Congressman Issa's blockbuster hearing would reveal that knowledge of this operation, which was part of a larger drug interdiction program, was not limited to a handful of bureaucrats in Phoenix, but included officials at the Federal Bureau of Investigation, Justice Department and Drug Enforcement Administration. Melson's subsequent testimony confirmed these allegations, and congressional investigators further discovered that some of the so-called kingpins of the smuggling operations may have actually been paid informants for the Federal Bureau of Investigation and/or the Drug Enforcement Administration – all unbeknownst to the ATF during the operation.

To answer to the question that opened this chapter, one has to ask another question: How does requiring gun dealers to report firearm sales prevent a crime that may occur six months or a year later? Why hold gun dealers and honest private citizens responsible for crime in another country when it is the very agency whose job it is to interdict illegal weapons that has allowed and even exacerbated the flow of guns across the nation's southern border? Why bother monitoring gun sales as a strategy to discourage illegal gun trafficking, if it is our own government that is enabling that same trafficking?

Gun prohibitionist defenders of the Obama administration were quick to launch efforts to deflect public attention away from the obvious. They tried to keep alive the false notion that gun shows, gun shops and gun laws in this country are responsible for allowing so many firearms to flow south. At every turn, they would obfuscate, attempt to shift the focus, and ultimately to try discrediting the information that was, in the final analysis, damning to the administration they so wanted to keep in power.

Early in 2011, after Sen. Grassley had been repeatedly stonewalled by the Justice Department and ATF on his inquiries, Rep. Issa stepped in to provide a crucial link in finding the truth. While Grassley, as ranking minority member of the Senate Judiciary Committee did not have the authority to issue subpoenas and launch full-scale investigations, Issa as a committee chairman did, and he used it. He sent congressional investigators to Arizona to interview whistleblowers and gun dealers, he subpoenaed documents from the ATF, and most importantly, he launched hearings into the gunrunning sting. What those hearings revealed was alarming.

The investigation revealed an administration, and particularly a Justice Department, that was at varying times either asleep at the wheel or so fundamentally dishonest about the depth of involvement that questions were raised about criminal liabilities.

What does this have to do with mandating the reporting of multiple sales of rifles and shotguns to the ATF?

Politically speaking, that proposal was nothing more than a smokescreen, designed to divert public attention away from the brutal fact that an agency of our own government had facilitated the arming of Mexican gangsters, and then tried to blame gun dealers and allegedly "weak" U.S. gun laws.

There is more to this debate than just Operation Fast and Furious. It is the continued effort of gun prohibitionists to track any and all firearms transactions, whether the retail sale of a rifle, shotgun or handgun to a customer, or even the gifting of a firearm from one family member to another. Many gun rights activists argue that the government has no business monitoring firearms ownership. It is none of the government's business what guns, or how many, a law-abiding citizen may own, they contend. Government should only enter the picture in the event a firearm is misused in a criminal act, many gun rights advocates insist.

But this pressure for firearms monitoring is nothing new. Gun prohibitionists have, over the years, tried one strategy after another in an attempt to discourage firearms ownership. Licensing and registration have been high on the list, but so also has the desire to regulate gun shows out of existence by requiring background checks on all transactions, including those conducted between private parties, which has been allowed under the federal Gun Control Act since it was passed in 1968.

Anti-gunners have adopted the piecemeal approach, having evidently determined some time ago that slow erosion of a civil right is the only way to accomplish its complete destruction. The gun prohibition movement learned long ago that trying to take too much too fast will result in a public backlash.

While a reporting requirement on multiple firearms sales may seem innocuous at first, because it would be structured to target repeated high volume purchases by known or suspected straw buyers, it would only be a matter of time before an amendment to the law would require reports of two firearms purchases by the same individual at one time, and then purchases of more than one firearm per week or month.

There is a "slippery slope" and the strongest denial of the slippery slope argument comes from those who intend to grease the skids, making the slope all that more slippery.

Regulations to discourage gun ownership make the job a little easier. Whether a person is required to submit to a background check in order to give, trade or sell a firearm to a known friend or family member, or to submit to a more formal process to purchase a firearm at retail, and then perhaps endure a waiting period, the goal is the same. Gun control advocates want fewer people to own firearms, and they have pushed regulations to make the process as difficult as possible.

It is not that large a leap from one-gun-per-month restrictions to one gun every six months or one gun a year. If a government hostile to private gun ownership can pass such a law, there really is nothing to prevent statutes limiting the number of firearms someone might own.

In the wake of Supreme Court rulings that the Second Amendment protects a fundamental individual civil right, it now has become a fertile environment for litigation challenging some of these laws and regulations. Government cannot place burdensome roadblocks in the way of people who merely wish to exercise a constitutionally-protected civil right.

However, there is nothing in either of the high court rulings that suggests government cannot limit the number of guns someone may buy or own.

One might also argue that monitoring gun sales is a means of establishing a *de facto* gun registry, albeit an admittedly incomplete one because there are so many firearms now in circulation that to get data on all of them is simply impossible.

Equally impossible, and implausible, was the ATF's purported goal of Operation Fast and Furious. The plan – if one can actually call it that – was to allow known or suspected gun runners and straw purchasers to put guns they bought at U.S. gun stores into circulation and track them back to Mexico with the intent of using the information to bring down a major cartel. The plan is preposterous from the outset, because firearms that cross the border into Mexico or any other foreign country are virtually impossible to track, especially if those guns are *knowingly* put into the hands of criminals.

As one ATF whistleblower told Congress, the next time anyone might see any of those guns after they have been taken from a gun shop is when they are recovered at the scene of a crime. There was no genuine tracking involved, despite claims to the contrary. Minor efforts to place GPS devices in some guns were failures. The operation got out of hand almost immediately, and stayed that way for months. It was only the slaying of a U.S. Border Patrol agent that resulted in the first arrest, followed about six weeks later by the indictment and arrests of 19 other suspects.

But instead of major cartel figures, every one of those arrested in connection with Fast and Furious was little more than a small-time operative. Instead of bringing down a cartel, this operation brought down the fury of Congress. By the time Congress became involved, some people were already running for cover.

Reporting gun sales, even multiple sales, does not "keep dealers honest" as the title of this chapter suggests. The overwhelming majority of firearms dealers are honest businessmen already, burdened by regulations that require legal knowledge to properly interpret at times, because one can actually get conflicting interpretations from different ATF spokespersons.

What's more, the courts have consistently held that firearms dealers, and gun makers, are not responsible for the misuse of their products by the end user. Doing so would be comparable to holding a car manufacturer or a car dealer responsible for a crime committed by someone weeks or months later while behind the wheel of a vehicle they sold.

A look at various state gun laws reveals many layers of requirements over and above those mandated by federal statute and regulations. Many so-called "dishonest" gun dealers are people who have simply made paperwork errors, but they are still considered violations under a set of guidelines so rigid that even minor infractions can create headaches. Truly criminal gun dealers get caught and prosecuted. At the very least they lose their licenses.

One might argue – and sound reasonable in the process – that there really is nothing wrong with requiring firearms retailers to report multiple sales of firearms. However, if someone passes a background check, why does it matter how many firearms that individual purchases?

What is really at stake here is not clamping down on suspected gunrunners, but in establishing a standard that will allow gun prohibitionists to take their campaign to the next level: Limiting the number and types of firearms someone may purchase, in a week, or a month and perhaps ultimately, in a calendar year.

One more step beyond that is a limit on the number of firearms a person may own.

This is, of course, the "slippery slope" argument, but a careful review of gun laws and how they have expanded over the past half-century should be all that is necessary to demonstrate that the slippery slope does exist.

For example, in California, so-called "assault weapons" were required to be registered, but then the law changed so that the state stopped accepting registrations for such guns, in effect creating a ban. Guns not registered by the deadline must be surrendered to law enforcement or moved out of state. (And don't get caught on the highway trying to move your unregistered semiautomatic rifle out of the state if it is not registered.)

If Operation Fast and Furious taught us anything, it was that the program, itself, was responsible for putting a lot of guns into the wrong hands. It is not typical that people walk into a gun shop with a wad of cash, purchase a dozen or more of the same kind of firearm and then walk out and put those guns in their car trunk, and then come back the next week and do it all over again.

Gun dealers will routinely tip off the ATF about this kind of purchase, without the necessity of passing a new law. In the case of Operation Fast and Furious, the investigation revealed that gun dealers repeatedly expressed their concerns about this project to the ATF, but officials there simply told them not to worry and to allow the transactions to be completed. Even field agents watching as the transactions occurred were ordered by their superiors to allow the suspects to leave the stores and drive away with the guns, which is counter to standard interdiction procedure that does not allow firearms to move into the illicit trafficking stream.

When it became an issue with some field agents, then-group VII supervisor David J. Voth sent out an e-mail to all concerned that said this:

> *I don't know what all the issues are but we are all adults, we are all professionals, and we have a (sic) exciting opportunity to use the biggest tool in our law enforcement tool box. If you don't think this is fun you're in the wrong line of work – period! This is the pinnacle of domestic U.S. law enforcement techniques. After this the tool bag is empty. Maybe the Maricopa County Jail is hiring detention officers and you can get paid $30,000 (instead of $100,000) to serve lunch to inmates all day...We need to get over this bump in the road once and for all and get on with the mission at hand. This can be the most fun you have with ATF, the only one limiting the amount of fun we have is you!*

As the investigation unfolded and investigative reporters dug into the story, more shocking revelations surfaced. Congressman Issa revealed that then Acting

ATF Director Melson had real-time access to a live camera in at least one Arizona gun shop so that he could observe suspected illegal gun transactions taking place as they happened, on his computer screen in his Washington, D.C. office. Melson, as noted earlier in this chapter, subsequently denied ever having actually utilized this live-camera link.

Virtually the entire management team in the Phoenix ATF field office was transferred and replaced. Many believed this amounted to an acknowledgement by the agency that something had gone terribly wrong, and that a correction was necessary. But was it enough?

Democrats on the Issa committee tried to redirect public attention away from the scandalous nature of the ATF operation, which critics were convinced had occurred with the full knowledge, if not the tacit approval, of higher-ups in the Obama administration. Ranking committee member Elijah E. Cummings, a Maryland anti-gunner, conducted a "forum" on the subject of illegal gun trafficking, at which he allowed one gun prohibitionist after another to testify. On the panel were Paul Helmke, then president of the Brady Campaign to Prevent Gun Violence, and Kristen Rand, legislative director of the Violence Policy Center.

Their solutions to the problem of ATF-sanctioned gun trafficking were right out of the gun control playbook.

According to Helmke, "We need to prohibit the sale of military-style semi-automatic assault weapons and assault clips."

The "assault clip" was a relatively new invention of terms by Helmke and the Brady camp. It alludes to the standard-capacity or extended capacity magazines for rifles and pistols that are commonly owned by recreational shooters and competitors, and varmint hunters. Now, it is not only firearms, but firearms components that are demonized by the anti-gun rights lobby.

Rand followed with a similar call for an "effective federal assault weapons ban." Likewise, she called for a ban on large capacity ammunition magazines, and for restrictions on the ownership of .50-caliber long-range target rifles.

"Virtually all of the guns terrorizing Mexico utilize high-capacity ammunition magazines that enable shooters to fire non-stop 20, 30, 50, or even 100 rounds of ammunition while allowing for quick reloading," she said

Actually, it is and was Mexican gunmen who have been terrorizing that country, and the guns they use come from various sources, including Central America and even China.

Mandating a requirement that American gun dealers report multiple sales of rifles is not going to hinder Mexican drug cartels from obtaining weapons from other international sources operating all over the world. Naturally, gun prohibition advocates do not care to hear that, and they will quickly respond that the overwhelming majority of firearms recovered by Mexican officials come from the United States, which is, as we noted earlier, a demonstrable falsehood.

With so many firearms flowing into Mexico from sources other than the United States, one is compelled to ask what difference it would make to victims in Mexico from all gun-related violence whether a firearms dealer in Arizona or New Mexico reported multiple sales of firearms as a mandate, when he or she probably already tipped off the ATF by telephone? One might add, especially if those guns were allowed to cross the border by an operation mounted by a federal government agency.

Still, in mid-2011, Deputy Attorney General James Cole issued the following statement, ordering the reporting of multiple sales of semi-automatic rifles with detachable magazines in four border states:

> *The international expansion and increased violence of transnational criminal networks pose a significant threat to the United States. Federal, state and foreign law enforcement agencies have determined that certain types of semi-automatic rifles - greater than .22 caliber and with the ability to accept a detachable magazine - are highly sought after by dangerous drug trafficking organizations*

and frequently recovered at violent crime scenes near the Southwest Border. This new reporting measure -- tailored to focus only on multiple sales of these types of rifles to the same person within a five-day period -- will improve the ability of the Bureau of Alcohol, Tobacco, Firearms and Explosives to detect and disrupt the illegal weapons trafficking networks responsible for diverting firearms from lawful commerce to criminals and criminal organizations. These targeted information requests will occur in Arizona, California, New Mexico, and Texas to help confront the problem of illegal gun trafficking into Mexico and along the Southwest Border.

Two days later, an amendment to the Justice Department's appropriation was added by Montana Congressman Denny Rehberg that prohibited the use of DOJ funds to operate the reporting program.

The reporting requirement was viewed by many as an administration attempt to deflect public attention away from the growing Fast and Furious scandal. In the midst of this, e-mail exchanges between ATF officials surfaced that fueled speculation that the real goal of Fast and Furious was not to find and arrest gun traffickers, but to bolster the ATF's demand for long gun reporting.

In an e-mail between Mark Chait, deputy ATF director for Field Operations, and William Newell, then special agent in charge in the Phoenix ATF office regarding an arrest a day earlier of an ex-convict with a truck load of firearms, Chait asked Newell, "can you see if these guns were all purchased from same FfL (sic) and at one time. We are looking at anecdotal cases to support a demand letter on long gun multiple sales."

Such exchanges reinforce the notion among many gun rights activists that the gun trafficking sting was actually an elaborate effort to "pad the numbers" of U.S.-origin guns recovered from crime scenes south of the border. The justification for such an effort would be that it bolsters the argument in favor of added restrictions on this nation's firearms dealers and gun owners. Making it even more believable was the report that President Obama had indicated to gun control proponents in early 2011 that he was working on new "gun safety" initiatives "under the radar."

In the final analysis, it is not gun dealers who need to be "kept honest" but an administration that has labored to prevent congressional investigators from getting to the bottom of a horribly concocted and disastrously executed "sting" that might never have gone unchecked except for the untimely death of a federal Border Patrol agent during a gun battle in the Arizona desert just days before Christmas 2010.

Twelve

WE SHOULD LIMIT THE NUMBER OF GUNS PEOPLE CAN BUY

Q. *What's wrong with limiting the number of guns someone can buy to one per month? Who needs more than that?*

Enacting limitations on any civil right, even or especially the right to keep and bear arms should be considered a civil rights outrage.

What purpose is served with a one-gun-per-month statute? Virginia Tech gunman Sueng Hui-Cho carefully spent time buying the two handguns he used by waiting a month between purchases. Seattle Jewish Federation gunman Naveed Afzal Haq bought his two pistols at different gun shops waiting between purchases.

Restrictive firearms statutes have demonstrated only one thing with certainty: They place a burden on law-abiding citizens and have not been shown to have prevented a single violent crime.

When Illinois lawmakers were debating a concealed carry measure in that state in 2011, the Associated Press reported that some Illinois anti-gunners pointed to the state's "significant information gaps" in the ability to "detect and screen out people with serious mental illnesses who might go on a shooting rampage."

Is the state's failure to maintain adequate records on certain individuals who may be disqualified from owning or possessing firearms a good enough reason to prevent millions of law-abiding citizens from exercising their right to bear arms?

In this nation, we do not punish the innocent for the crimes of the guilty or even advocate that as a rational policy except where firearms are concerned.

We do not hold every driver in the country responsible for people who drive drunk and cause traffic accidents.

We do not punish all members of the working press when some reporter commits an act of plagiarism, or authors a report that is later proven to be a fabrication.

Yet we insist that all gun owners be screened with a background check, and in some states require them to have some type of permit to even own a firearm. Restrictive gun laws in New York, New Jersey, Maryland, Illinois and California could not rationally be said to have prevented crime or kept violent crime rates low, because that is demonstrably false. Crime rates in those states, compared to other states with high rates of gun ownership and lower rates of violent crime, tell the tale.

Limiting gun purchases to one per month is seen by many firearms civil rights advocates as being the top of a slippery slope that could ultimately lead to limiting people to one gun every three months, and then one every six months, or one per year. Proponents of such laws would argue that this does not eliminate the right to keep and bear arms; it simply limits the number of arms someone can keep and bear. It is a ludicrous argument, of course, but in the mind of a devoted gun prohibitionist, this is a "reasonable" and "sensible" approach to a nasty problem.

The South Carolina experience probably best underscores the foolishness of such laws. For many years, South Carolina had a one-gun-per-month statute (as do

California, Virginia and Maryland), which was accurately described by the National Rifle Association as a "gun rationing" law. The state imposed the gun rationing law in 1975, ostensibly as a means of stopping the flow of illegal guns to New York City. After the law took effect, violent crime went up in both New York City, and in South Carolina.

In the 1990s, according to a brief history of the South Carolina law found on the NRA website, violent crime began declining nationally, except in Washington, D.C. which was supposed to have been the main beneficiary of a similar gun rationing law in neighboring Virginia, the NRA observed.

Maryland imposed the one-gun-per-month regulation in 1998, but the homicide rate in Baltimore and the robbery rate across the state went up, not down.

In 2004, South Carolina finally reversed course, and the law was repealed, having not accomplished anything tangible in the process. The sky did not fall, nor did South Carolina streets turn red with rivers of flowing blood. And there is still violent crime in the City of New York. Illicit gun traffickers did not appear to have slowed their activities down.

Two years later, in a report published by the *Philadelphia Inquirer*, the effectiveness of these gun rationing laws was called into question. The newspaper revealed that two studies, one published in 2005 by Injury Prevention and the other done in 2001 by Johns Hopkins Center for Gun Policy and Research, were hardly glowing endorsements of gun rationing, yet neither of these entities can be described as being philosophically pro-gun.

In the more recent case, the newspaper reported, a study done by a team of physicians from the University of Washington that analyzed data from 1979 to 1998, revealed that "laws restricting purchases had had no measureable impact" on crime. The earlier study at Johns Hopkins did reveal "a slight decrease in gun violence associated with Maryland's one-gun law."

But what does that mean, really? The *Inquirer* story further revealed that Baltimore, and Richmond, Virginia had homicide rates that were "among the highest in the country." The newspaper also confirmed that all three states with still-existing gun rationing laws "had homicide rates above the national average – slightly above in California and Virginia, well above in Maryland."

"With only California, Virginia and Maryland having such laws," the newspaper observed, "there isn't much evidence to be had. What is available raises questions about the effect of limiting individuals to one handgun purchase every 30 days."

Naturally, proponents of the limit insisted the absence of solid data supporting their position is no reason to abandon the strategy. Perhaps they believe if they keep trying the same failed program over and over, they will eventually get a different result, which suits their pre-conceived notion and their political agenda.

Anti-gunners should never be underestimated in their penchant for proposing laws or regulations that would be considered preposterous if applied to any other Constitutionally-protected civil right.

In 2011, a candidate for mayor in the City of Baltimore proposed a $1 tax on every cartridge someone purchases in the city as a means of discouraging people in the city from using guns in violent crime or irresponsibly fire guns at holidays such as the Fourth of July or New Year's.

Democrat Otis Rolley offered his suggestion because, he explained, "Increasing the cost of guns won't work, because many criminals don't purchase new guns, and they can be borrowed or even rented in some areas."

Like so much that is said by anti-gunners who simply dislike firearms and have really no functional knowledge about guns or crime, Rolley's remark is simply ludicrous. He honestly believed that criminals could rent firearms. He seems to understand that criminals do not buy brand new firearms at retail in most cases, but that's where the disconnect with reality sets in, because he evidently did not understand that criminals typically *steal* the guns they use, or they get them from someone else who steals guns. They do not rent firearms.

As noted in an earlier chapter, criminals rarely obtain guns from gun shows, and they most certainly do not simply steal a gun and then go purchase ammunition. They usually steal the ammunition when they steal the firearm. Sometimes, as when a criminal steals a gun from a policeman – as was the case in late 2004 when someone stole former Seattle Police Chief Gil Kerlikowske's 9mm Glock pistol from his parked department-issue car on a downtown Seattle street – the gun is already loaded.

Levying a $1 tax per cartridge on ammunition is not going to prevent anyone from indiscriminately firing a gun in the neighborhood on a holiday or any other time. What this does accomplish, though, is to financially penalize law-abiding hunters, recreational shooters and citizens who own firearms for personal protection. It might also help push firearms and ammunition retailers out of the city, which seems to be a fine idea among urban anti-gunners, though it might be somewhat self-defeating since they would lose the revenue that they would be spending on entitlement programs or other non-essential government services.

In short, it is a liberal exercise in hypocrisy; condemn gun violence and firearms foolishness, yet figure out a way to fatten the government's bank account in the process.

Rolley, much the same as officials in the City of Chicago did after they lost the *McDonald v. City of Chicago* lawsuit on Second Amendment grounds, elicited the myopic viewpoint that if he limited firearms or ammunition access inside the city, people would be stymied.

To the contrary, criminals would simply go outside the city and obtain their arms and ammunition, without the tax penalty. One does not hurt criminals by inconveniencing their potential victims.

The idea was so preposterous that it was publicly ridiculed by the Citizens Committee for the Right to Keep and Bear Arms, a national organization based in Bellevue, Washington. They issued a statement that said "Rolley's trolley has left the tracks."

Limiting the number of firearms a person can legally purchase as a means of fighting crime overlooks the obvious. There is no such limitation placed on the number of guns someone can steal, and as has been demonstrated far too many times, determined gun thieves will steal from various sources, including the police and even the FBI. In the latter case, often times the thieves get far more than anyone cares to acknowledge: Fully-automatic firearms and lots of ammunition and accessories.

Ostensibly, the one-gun-per-month philosophy was pandered as a means of discouraging illegal firearms trafficking from states with more reasonable firearms laws to states where gun laws are very restrictive. Does this mean that all of those guns were falling into criminal hands?

Not hardly; many people in states like New York or New Jersey, and even in cities like Chicago and Washington, D.C. who have been essentially disarmed by local gun laws will occasionally arm themselves anyway by purchasing guns for their own protection from people who are not licensed dealers. The authorities know this, and so does the firearms community.

Perhaps the best example of this involved the 80-year-old Korean War veteran living in Chicago who purchased a handgun several months before the Supreme Court handed down the McDonald ruling, and used that pistol to defend himself and his family against a neighborhood thug in May 2010, about a month prior to the high court ruling. We discussed this story in Chapter 2, but bring it up again to illustrate a different element of the story. The man he killed, Anthony "Big Ant" Nelson, fired a shot at the octogenarian war vet and his wife as they lay in bed. Nelson, as we explained earlier, was not permitted by law to possess a gun, but when did that small detail ever stop a criminal intent on mayhem? It certainly has not stopped other felons in Chicago or anywhere else.

When his intended victim fired back, to Nelson's terminal surprise, he did so with a handgun that *was not registered inside the city*, and therefore was being kept there illegally. Nelson was killed, yet the older man was never charged with a crime.

The would-be victim later told reporters that he had been robbed several months earlier, and had made a decision – regardless of the city law at the time – that this would not happen to him again. It was legal at the time for Chicago residents with a Firearms Owner Identification (FOID) Card to own a handgun but keep it outside the city. It was also widely known that many Chicago residents, some of them prominent citizens, routinely ignored the law and brought their handguns home.

This case perfectly illustrates why otherwise law-abiding citizens will knowingly keep firearms illegally in their homes. They know that in a life-or-death situation, police will never arrive in time to save the day. It is not known whether the old gentleman ever replaced the pistol that Chicago police took from him, and one can presume anything one wants. While the man was never publicly identified by police because he was described as a crime victim who acted in self-defense, everyone in the neighborhood knew him, and applauded him for having removed a threat to the entire community.

To have charged him with a crime would have been political suicide for the Cook County prosecutor, and everybody knows it. With the pending *McDonald* ruling by the Supreme Court only weeks away – and everyone was anticipating a majority opinion that would strike down the Chicago handgun ban – only an anti-gun zealot willing to face the moral outrage of his constituents would have pursued a criminal charge.

Limiting people to one gun purchase monthly can defeat ardent gun collectors, competitors and other citizens with entirely legitimate reasons to be making a multiple purchase (i.e. the man who purchases matching shotguns for himself and his spouse; the father who does the same for himself and a son or daughter; the competitor whose firearm malfunctions or breaks down; a collector with the opportunity to purchase matched sets of a particular gun model, the hunter whose firearms are lost or stolen, and so forth). In a society where keeping and bearing arms is a recognized constitutional right, one should not be required to demonstrate any kind of "need" just to exercise that right, as we discussed in Chapter 8.

As noted earlier in this chapter, gun prohibitionists like the idea of limiting people to one firearm purchase per month. They may claim many different reasons for this, such as fighting crime and preventing illegal gun trafficking, but what they will never discuss is that imposing such a limit is primarily for the purpose of conditioning the public to the idea that such limits are both acceptable and constitutional. They are neither.

The same logical disconnect applies to the aforementioned proposal by the Maryland mayoral candidate to levy a per-cartridge tax on ammunition. What if that same principle had been suggested for taxing the printed word? What would the mainstream press have said? How would editorial boards across the state have reacted to the proposition that government could institute a $1 per word tax on newspaper editorial pages?

The reaction would have been swift and entirely negative. Newspaper editorial boards would have denounced such a silly idea as unconstitutional, and editorially browbeaten the candidate into political oblivion.

An attack on one civil right is a threat to all civil rights, for if it is perceived that one right is vulnerable to this sort of demagoguery, it will not be long before some other right falls under this form of political assault.

Nobody who claims to believe in democracy or civil rights should ever advocate adoption of statutes or regulations that empower the government to place a limit on the exercise of a fundamental civil right outside of penalties for criminal convictions. Certainly, prohibiting convicted violent offenders from possessing firearms seems a prudent limitation on the right to keep and bear arms, but limiting someone from merely shopping for firearms – when that individual can pass a background check – has no rational basis. This is a civil impairment on the exercise of a civil right.

None of this matters to the gun prohibition lobby. Indeed, throughout the history of the gun ban movement

– for that is really what gun control has always been about – prohibitionists have twisted data and ignored evidence that did not fit their agenda in order to sell the notion that fewer firearms in the hands of law abiding citizens would somehow make society safer, when in fact, quite the opposite has been shown repeatedly to be the case.

Handguns were banned and long guns were severely restricted in Great Britain following the Dunblane Massacre in 1996. Crime rates have risen dramatically in the United Kingdom ever since, including gun- and knife-related crime.

After Chicago and Washington, D.C. banned handguns, the homicide rates in both cities skyrocketed.

States with the strictest gun control laws have experienced higher overall crime rates.

It is obvious that gun laws which impose restrictions on law-abiding citizens who would never consider breaking a law have had no impact on criminals. This is because social predators ignore such laws and operate outside of them. Why this is consistently lost on gun prohibitionists has never been rationally explained.

Anti-gunners are fearful of firearms and honestly believe that the fewer of them around, even in the hands of law-abiding citizens, the better it will be for their personal safety. Perhaps that is the heart of this great debate. Gun prohibitionists are concerned about *their* safety rather than public safety or the ability of their neighbors to ward off a violent criminal attack.

It's *their* comfort zone we are ultimately talking about; *their* peace of mind in a dangerous environment.

Facts simply do not matter to such individuals. They would have the rest of us conform to their standards, even if to do so translates to a surrender of our communities to the criminal element.

This is why the gun prohibition lobby will never give up, never seriously engage in a "middle ground" conversation and never acknowledge that their opinions and strategies have been wrong and have consistently failed to prevent crime. For the gun prohibition lobby, each new law they could pass during the heyday of gun control was always "a good first step." There was never a "last step." No matter what they got, they invariably wanted more.

It is time to take a new direction. The gun control movement has, in the final analysis, given this country little more than a body count; a social experiment in usually involuntary unilateral disarmament that produced lots of unarmed casualties – later exploited by gun ban proponents as proof that even stricter measures were needed – while leaving good people at a distinct disadvantage to bad people.

Advocating weakness and submissiveness to criminals has never worked. People have been robbed, raped, beaten and murdered, and criminals have gone free to do it all over again the next night. In the wake of the mayhem, all gun prohibitionists could do is demand even greater restrictions on law-abiding citizens who want to, or already do, own a firearm for personal protection.

This is why the gun ban lobby has lost so much traction over the past few years. The pendulum of public sentiment has started swinging back the other way. Abraham Lincoln once observed that "You can fool all of the people some of the time, and some of the people all of the time, but you can't fool all of the people all of the time."

People have awakened to the modern reality that one does not fight crime by surrendering neighborhoods or households or businesses to the criminal element.

In the process, people have realized that the gun prohibition lobby, for all its slick semantics about "gun safety" and "common sense" laws, really wants to disarm the public and erase the Second Amendment.

In the battle of good against evil, these people are shooting blanks.

Thirteen

AMERICA SHOULD PATTERN ITS GUN LAWS AFTER EUROPE

Q. *Why can't we follow the example of European nations with gun laws that prevent the kinds of crimes we see here in the United States?*

Even before and certainly after several high-profile shooting incidents in the United States over the past two decades – incidents that include the tragic school shootings at Columbine High School in Colorado and the Virginia Tech massacre – gun prohibitionists have argued that America should adopt the same kinds of restrictive gun laws that are currently in effect in European nations.

These measures, we were assured, would cut down on violence by limiting access to firearms. While the arguments in favor of such gun control measures were put forth, those advocating these new restrictions were being deceitful at best and quite possibly delusional.

Strict European gun regulations have not prevented outbreaks of violence, and some of the worst mass shootings over the past half-century have occurred not in the United

States, but in nations with some of the toughest firearms regulations on the planet.

When it comes to mass shootings, not even Virginia Tech can rival the carnage wrought by Norwegian gunman Anders Behring Breivik. After he set off a bomb in downtown Oslo, he traveled a short distance to Utoya Island, where he began a 90-minute shooting spree that left dozens dead, while police were delayed in their response because they could not get a seaworthy boat. When the shooting was done, and authorities had an opportunity to do an accurate body count, they determined that Breivik had killed more than 70 people, twice the number murdered by Seung-Hui Cho at Virginia Tech.

Norway's gun laws are strict, and what was doubly stunning about the crime was that Breivik was a home-grown terrorist, and that Norway experiences relatively little violent crime, compared to other nations. In Norway, shotguns, rifles and handguns are strictly regulated. One must state in writing his or her reasons for wanting to own a firearm, and guns must be stored under lock and key, and police have the authority to visit the home of a gun owner to confirm that the laws and regulations are being followed.

Under Norway's gun laws, "only sober and responsible" persons over age 18 may obtain a Norwegian gun license, and for handguns, the minimum age is 21. Gun rights advocates were quick to note that the inability to mount a defense against Breivik's attack is one reason the body count was so high in July 2011.

Of course, the Norway slaughter is not the only mass murder to occur in Europe, and if this situation proves anything, it is that the arguments of gun prohibition are hollow, indeed, against the determination of an individual bent on wreaking havoc.

The Jokela school massacre in the Tuusula municipality of Finland in November 2007 is a stark reminder that even strict gun laws cannot prevent someone from committing a crime, and, lacking clairvoyance, firearms dealers or government officials cannot predict whether someone will go on a killing spree six months or a year in the future.

In Jokela, 18-year-old Pekka-Eric Auvinen used a pistol to murder eight people and wound a ninth person in the foot before turning the gun on himself. He had opened fire almost immediately, and after the school went into lockdown with barricaded doors to the classrooms, he reportedly walked the hallways declaring that a revolution had begun. He shot the school principal and the school nurse, killing both. He died later that night in a Helsinki hospital from a head wound.

Auvinen had only gotten his government-issued gun license three weeks prior to the shooting. A registered member of the Helsinki Shooting Club, he legally purchased the .22-caliber semiautomatic pistol in October. He had no prior criminal record.

In March 2009 in Winnenden, a community in southern Germany, 17-year-old Tim Kretschmer, a former student at the Albertville Realschule, walked into the building and opened fire. Before he was finished, he had killed 15 people including three teachers and nine students. He also killed three citizens before turning the gun on himself. All but one of his victims was female.

His spree was a bit different, in that he left the school, shot a passer-by, hijacked an automobile and drove to another community about 20 miles away, where he left his stolen car, went to a car dealership, killed two more people and then killed himself as local police closed in.

Kretschmer used one of his father's legally-own pistols, a 9mm Beretta, in his rampage. Authorities later suggested that the teen wanted to kill as many people as possible.

Germany has very tight firearms regulations and when German authorities visited his father's home, they found all of his guns securely stored. The elder Kretschmer was a member of a local gun club. The gunman left no suicide note or any other explanation about his motivation.

Another 17-year-old mounted a bloody attack in Sollies-le-Pont and Cuers in France in September 1995. He killed 16 people and wounded several others before taking his own life.

The Dunblane, Scotland massacre in March 1996 was the catalyst for the adoption of very stringent gun laws in the United Kingdom. In that attack, 16 students and their teacher were slain before the gunman, described as a "deranged gun collector" in various accounts, shot himself to death.

But the tough gun laws adopted to prevent another Dunblane didn't do that at all. In June 2010, a British taxi driver named Derrick Bird opened fire in Lamplugh, and then traveled to several different local communities, shooting and killing people until he racked up a body count of 12 people and wounded 11 others.

The 52-year-old Bird left 30 different crime scenes in his wake, using two firearms. After the shooting, Bird walked into a wooded area and took his own life.

Researcher John Lott noted in a retrospective about European mass shootings that "It may be a surprise to those who believe in gun control that Germany was home to three of the five worst attacks. Though not quite as tight as the U.K.'s regulations, Germany's gun-control laws are some of the most restrictive in Europe. German gun licenses are valid for only three years, and to obtain one, the person must demonstrate such hard-to-define characteristics as trustworthiness, and must also convince authorities that he needs a gun. This is on top of prohibitions on gun ownership for those with mental disorders, drug or alcohol addictions, violent or aggressive tendencies, or felony convictions."

According to Lott, the first decade of the 21st Century saw several mass shootings across Europe, from Italy to Finland. There was one in September 2001 in Zug, Switzerland that left 14 members of a cantonal parliament dead. The following month, a French railway worker opened fire at an intersection in Tours, France killing four people and wounding ten others.

In February 2002, three people were killed and one was wounded in a shooting in Freising, Germany. In March

2002, another French gunman killed eight members of the Nanterre city council after their regular meeting. The next month in Erfurt, Germany, a former school student came to a secondary school there and fatally shot 18 people.

The French incident was particularly interesting because the 33-year-old gunman Richard Durn waited for several hours until the meeting was over to open fire. It later turned out that he had been an occasional spectator at these meetings. He was armed with a pair of Glock semiautomatic pistols and apparently a Smith & Wesson .357 Magnum revolver according to some reports. After the shooting, the gunman reportedly was tackled because his guns were empty. He repeatedly uttered "kill me, kill me" after he was taken down.

As Joseph P. Tartaro, executive editor of *Gun Week,* a firearms publication that is something of the "newspaper of record" for the firearms community, wrote following the 2002 shootings in France and Germany, "Gun control advocates in the U.S. frequently point to European models to support their claims that restrictions on firearms acquisition and possession will reduce gun-related crime and mass murders. In support of their arguments, they bend the statistics they trot out to propagandize the public.

"But in recent years, they have been downplaying their European models," Tartaro continued, "because in contrast to the continuing decline in violent crimes in the U.S., crime has been rising rapidly in such paragons of gun control as Britain, France and Germany. Then they become strangely silent."

Tartaro later noted in the same article that, "France's President Jacques Chirac and Prime Minister Lionel Jospin rushed to the crime scene to denounce the shooting. The reason the national politicians hurried to the scene and before TV cameras was because the rate of violent crime in France—with and without guns—has been rising so fast that it is a top issue in the current presidential election campaign in that nation."

Chirac and Jospin were running against each other in the elections that spring.

In November 2006, another "former student" in Emsdetten, Germany launched a rampage that left 11 people dead at his high school. Two years later, a gunman shot and killed ten people at a college in Kauhajoki, Finland. In that incident, 22-year-old Matti Juhani Saari used a .22-caliber Walther pistol on all of his victims before turning the gun on himself. The massacre unfolded at the Seinajoki University of Applied Sciences. There are several more incidents in which European gunmen killed multiple victims, often before turning the guns on themselves. This pretty much leaves in tatters the argument that European firearms laws are much better than gun laws in the United States in terms of preventing mass shooting incidents. It also puts the lie to the argument that mass shootings are something of an American phenomenon because of our so-called lax gun laws.

In an article he wrote for *National Review Online,* Lott noted, "Large multiple-victim public shootings are exceedingly rare events, but they garner massive news attention, and the misperceptions they produce are hard to erase.

"When I have been interviewed by foreign journalists," he recalled, "even German ones, they usually start off by asking why multiple-victim public shootings are such an American problem. And of course, they are astonished when I remind them of the attacks in their own countries and point out that this is not an American problem, it is a universal problem, but with a common factor: The attacks occur in public places where civilians are banned from carrying guns."

That problem was amplified in the Norway massacre because, as the *New York Times* reported, "By law, Norwegian police officers must have authorization from their chief to gain access to a firearm, but they have rarely needed to ask, until recently."

"Violent crime has been steadily increasing," the *Times* confirmed, "jolting a society used to leaving doors unlocked and children to play without fear. Coupled with growing criticism over the police's slow response time to the attacks and confusion about the death toll, which was lowered...to 76 from 93, there are growing questions about whether the police are equipped to deal with the challenges."

The newspaper also revealed that, "It took police SWAT units more than an hour to reach the camp, on Utoya Island, after reports of the shooting came in. Officers had to drive to the shore across from the site of the shooting attack, and use boats to get to the island. A police helicopter was unable to get off the ground; news crews that reached the island by air could only watch as the gunman continued the massacre."

The Winnenden, Germany massacre shows that a gunman will get his hands on a firearm, even if he must steal it from his father. The Utoya Island massacre in Norway underscores what Lott tells European reporters, and what the firearms community has long maintained: Mass shootings are far more successful in environments where people cannot fight back, and that doesn't differ from one country to the next. In Norway, even the police could not fight back, thus allowing the gunman 90 minutes to complete his orgy of homicide.

Making the problem even worst on Utoya Island, the gunman was dressed as a policeman. One of his first victims, according to the *New York Times*, was a genuine policeman, who was not armed.

These cases also illustrate another fact: One cannot accurately profile such gunmen and predict with any degree of certainty that a specific individual will or will not become a problem. The European shootings involved teenagers, 20-something people and an older taxi driver. Try to pull a demographic common denominator out of that.

In the years since England adopted its post-Dunblane gun laws, violent crime has actually risen across the United Kingdom. Even newspapers there have *editorialized about the problems, not only involving firearms but also knives.*

If this demonstrates anything, it is that criminals will arm themselves with whatever weapon they can obtain.

Trying to legislate against the criminal mind is virtually impossible, because they will invariably find a way to overcome any limitations placed on law-abiding citizens. After all, they are criminals. Breaking the law is what they do for a living, and quite often they are good at it.

Yet the myth persists that European gun laws are far better than American gun laws, and that they prevent the kinds of crimes faced by people in the United States. This philosophy is probably what is guiding many of the people involved in a United Nations effort to adopt an international gun control treaty on small arms, which the United States has opposed because any such treaty faces the very real potential of running headlong into the Second Amendment.

There is a genuine concern about this issue; so much so that a dozen Democrat senators and 45 Republicans in mid-summer 2011 advised President Barack Obama and Secretary of State Hillary Rodham Clinton in separate letters that they wanted this country's United Nations delegation to back away from a U.N. international gun control treaty effort that was being supported by the president.

The Democrat letter made it clear that "an Arms Trade Treaty that does not protect ownership of civilian firearms will fail in the Senate. Our firearm freedoms are not negotiable."

The Republican senators further advised the administration that "the establishment of any sort of international gun registry that could impede upon the privacy rights of law-abiding gun owners is a non-starter."

But an international arms trade treaty will not stop mass shootings any more than background checks – which were passed by Tucson, Arizona gunman Jared Lee Loughner and Virginia Tech gunman Seung-Hui Cho – have prevented such outrages. Nor have restrictive laws such as those adopted by foreign nations, which do not have Second Amendment provisions in their constitutions, prevented mass murderers from carrying out their deeds.

Yet gun prohibitionists adhere to the Utopian *fantasy* that such laws make society safer, even though there is an international body count that clearly proves otherwise.

Faced with the option of submitting to execution by a madman, or having the tools to fight back and perhaps save not only yourself but many others, which choice would you prefer?

Epilogue

DELIBERATELY SHOOTING BLANKS

Dishonesty has always been an important ingredient, if not the cornerstone, of gun prohibition rhetoric, and as this book was being prepared for publication, a story that appeared in the *Salt Lake Tribune* perhaps best underscores why the gun owning public has come to never expect fair or even objective reporting from major newspapers, even those in the heart of "gun country."

However, there is another example, from Detroit, Michigan, that levels the playing field, as we will momentarily explain. But first, let us deal with the *Salt Lake Tribune's* troubling article.

Sensationally headlined "Utah revokes record number of concealed gun permits," the actual report discussed how a change in the state law resulted in revocation, or nullification, of Utah concealed carry permits that had been obtained by non-state residents for a variety of reasons, none of which involved any commission of a crime.

Yet, to read the headline, one might quickly presume that a lot of people had lost their gun carry permits because they had run afoul of the law.

The deceptiveness of the headline was even more problematic, because the story revealed that out of more than 321,000 permits issued by the State of Utah, during the previous six months, the state's Bureau of Criminal Identification had revoked a paltry 539 permits. Yes, this was a "record" number compared to the total of 523 revocations posted in the previous year, but when compared to the total number of permits issued by the Beehive State, the number of revocations is less than 0.02 %.

Big deal; tempest in a teapot; call it anything you will, up to and including crass sensationalism and deceptive reporting. The facts about this story were far less significant than the newspaper's screaming headline attempted to portray.

According to the *Tribune's* article, "A law signed by Gov. Gary Herbert...requiring applicants from other states seeking a Utah concealed-weapon permit to obtain one from their home state first. Previously, there was no such requirement, making Utah's concealed-weapon permit an attractive option for those in states that some view as having more stringent training requirements or that charge more for their license.

"Phil Leiker, firearms investigator with the Bureau of Criminal Identification, said the crush of applicants has been largely unprecedented. And with the volume came a proportional number of revocations, which are done in cases in which a license holder shows up in the criminal database for violations ranging from domestic violence to armed robbery."

Of course, a tiny number of people will always show up in a database as being disqualified for having a concealed carry license. Take any cross-section of the population and that same result will be seen. There is nothing earth-shattering in such a revelation.

But other people whose permit applications were rejected simply did not have a permit from their home state, quite possibly because they live in states where authorities still have broad discretion to arbitrarily deny such carry permits. New Jersey and New York are among those states, and Illinois has no concealed carry statute, yet law-abiding Illinois residents could, until the change in Utah's law, go through the state's course and qualify for a non-resident permit. Likewise, California residents applied.

Such newspaper reporting and editing is not the result of an honest error, it is deliberately misleading and newspaper managers know it. This is much in the same reporting vein as the *New York Times* avoiding at every turn reporting that the Fort Hood massacre suspect was a Muslim, while it was quick to identify the Norway massacre gunman as having "right wing" views.

This kind of sensationalism, when there is very little solid ground for such reportage, is a key element in the campaign of gun owner demonization that has been carried on for decades in the United States. Half-truths and whole lies contribute nothing to an honest discussion about firearms civil rights under the U.S. Constitution and various state constitutions that have specific right-to-bear-arms tenets.

Perhaps as distressing, and non-contributory to the cause of gun rights, are those in the firearms community who are self-styled "mavericks" and "outlaws" who either ignore or outright defy state and federal firearms laws, and then have the audacity to claim some higher constitutional ground when they are prosecuted for violating known statutes, such as dealing in firearms without a license, engaging in "straw-man" purchases for associates they know to be disqualified from owning firearms, or deliberately selling firearms to people who acknowledge they cannot legally own guns.

These people are not crusaders or martyrs, they are lawbreakers, and like the managers of newspapers who deliberately misguide readers with deceptive headlines, these outlaw gun "activists" typically know they are breaking the law. When they run afoul of the law, they are hoisted by anti-gunners as typical examples of people in the firearms community, when they certainly are not. Indeed, law-abiding gun owners disdain such people.

Yet, in terms of numbers, such miscreants constitute a miniscule fraction of the millions of law-abiding gun owners who have never entertained the notion of deliberately violating the law. They have been, of course, working within the system to change laws that have placed them under undue burdens, and in recent years, they have pursued legal action in the courts. The hallmarks of this effort are, of course, the Supreme Court rulings in *District of Columbia v. Dick Anthony Heller* and *McDonald v. City of Chicago*. These cases have opened the doors for more and broader challenges to questionable firearms laws that, by no small surprise, are typically supported by newspaper editorial boards and gun prohibition organizations that seek to keep law abiding citizens disarmed.

Neither side in the great firearms rights debate is completely pure. It is incumbent upon those in the gun rights movement to endeavor toward the higher road, and to play it squarely, leaving the gun prohibition lobby and their media elite cheerleaders and enablers to wallow in deception.

Another newspaper, the *Detroit Free Press*, endeavored to get it right, however, leading many in the firearms community to hold out some hope that perhaps newsrooms are changing. On the tenth anniversary of Michigan's adoption of a reformed concealed carry statute, the newspaper published a two-part analysis headlined "10 years after concealed weapons law, unclear why many in state were gun-shy."

What the *Free Press* reported might have been considered blasphemy a dozen years earlier, when gun prohibitionists held much more political sway. "Ten years after Michigan made it much easier for its citizens to get a license to carry a concealed gun," the newspaper reported, "predictions of widespread lawless behavior and bloodshed have failed to materialize.

> *Today, nearly 276,000 -- or about four out of every 100 eligible adult Michiganders -- are licensed.*
> *During the debate, opponents of the change warned of gun-toting, trigger-happy citizens loose on the streets.*

> *But violent crimes have been rare among carrying a concealed weapon license holders. Only 2% of license holders have been sanctioned for any kind of misbehavior, State Police records show.*
>
> *Still, anti-gun activists say changing the law was a grave mistake. The Brady Campaign to Prevent Gun Violence Web site describes state reforms like the one enacted in Michigan as "a recipe for disaster."*
>
> *Michigan's prosecuting attorneys association led the push against changing the law in 2001. Today, Ionia County Prosecutor Ronald Schafer, president of the group, says it's hard to remember what the fuss was about.*
>
> *I think you can look back and say, "It was a big nothing."*

Particularly interesting is the paragraph detailing the position of the Brady Campaign, which was proven so wrong by calling Michigan's law "a recipe for disaster." This is a perfect example of the deliberately misleading rhetoric discussed throughout this book that has become the standard fodder for the Brady group and its like-minded friends in the gun prohibition lobby. One might go so far as to declare their position delusional.

It is certainly disingenuous, as the *Detroit Free Press* continued to report in the second half of its two-part series. In that revealing story, the newspaper noted, "Some of what passes for research and analysis of the effect of permissive concealed weapons laws on crime and violence is pretty crude."

The newspaper detailed the misleading rhetoric of the "anti-gun Violence Policy Center" (VPC) found on its Web page dubbed "Concealed Carry Killers." According to the *Free Press*, the VPC's examples of people who killed did not pass the credibility test.

> *It (VPC) purports to tally the carnage that results when states, such as Michigan, authorize*

ordinary citizens under most circumstances to be licensed to carry concealed guns," the newspaper said.

Concealed carry licensees "routinely" kill cops, perpetrate mass murders and other gun homicides, writes VPC. The center counted 308 "Private Citizens Killed By Concealed Carry Killer" since 2007. A lot of them -- 78 -- were Michiganders.

However, the newspaper took a closer look at the data than the VPC probably would have imagined and what it uncovered was revealing.

"A closer look at VPC's data doesn't necessarily confirm a CCW crime nightmare scenario," the *Free Press* explained. "The overwhelming majority of Michigan victims the center cites (62) were licensees who committed suicide. Michigan's concealed weapons law requires the State Police to report annually on deaths by suicide of license holders. But the reports contain no information about how the licensee died or whether a firearm was involved."

And this was perhaps the most devastating revelation uncovered by the newspaper: "Several other 'victims' in the VPC report appear to have been criminals themselves, shot attempting to rob legally armed citizens. But with 276,000 concealed pistol license holders, even the unscrubbed VPC numbers hardly establish evidence of a crime wave."

What it does establish – without the newspaper coming right out and saying so – is that the VPC engages in prevarication. And one must wonder just whose side the VPC is on, when it apparently uses statistics that include the justifiably-shot criminals whose outlaw behavior was at the core of the movement ten years earlier to amend the state's carry laws, thus allowing law-abiding citizens to arm themselves for the purpose of self-defense.

There will always be a criminal element, no matter what laws are passed, and no matter how effectively they are enforced. Likewise, there will never be a sufficient police presence to eliminate crime. That doesn't happen even in a police state, and that is not what the United States is, or ever will be so long as citizens remember that liberty and freedom are the foundations upon which our system of laws, checks and balances are built.

Alas, there will also always be an element in society that seeks – for whatever reason – to force the rest of us to conform to their narrow philosophy. They can never achieve this Utopian fairy tale without unilateral public disarmament, and they know it. People with the ability to resist can never be completely subjugated.

Gun prohibitionists, as illustrated by the examples above and earlier in this book, cling to the notion that an armed citizenry is a "recipe for disaster" while they twist data to further their own ends. When a newspaper does its job and reveals such fakery, it is a public service that is long overdue.

In a free society, there is always room for reasonable, rational and responsible debate of any issue. It is only when the political arguments stray into the realm of agenda fulfillment and philosophical monopoly that perspectives are lost, it not voluntarily abandoned.

The right to keep and bear arms is a fundamental, Constitutionally-protected civil right that is much broader than firearms prohibitionists will ever acknowledge. It is the "insurance policy" in our Bill of Rights that guarantees the defense and perpetuation of other rights, for without the ability to defend those rights – with force if necessary – they are little more than words on paper.

Fact and common sense are the ammunition in the battle to protect our firearms civil rights. Deception, innuendo, half-truths and outright falsehoods are the tools of those who would erode and ultimately erase our firearms freedoms. Those who deal in such habits and practices will always be shooting blanks.